sound✓check

The Basics of Sound and Sound Systems

ISBN 0-7935-3559-X

HAL•LEONARD™
CORPORATION

7777 W. BLUEMOUND RD. P.O. BOX 13819 MILWAUKEE, WI 53213

Introduction

I began playing music in a small Missouri bar at the age of twelve. As a singer /guitarist I fronted a band with two blind 13-year-olds who played guitar and bass. Our guitarist's dad played drums. As a novelty act (and an illegal one at that) we performed old standards and country tunes. Second channels of Magnatone and Kustom guitar amps brought our three part harmonies to audiences. The Radio Shack high impedance microphones always produced feedback, but none of us really cared. Besides, we didn't know what to do about it.

Fast Forward.

I moved on to a decent cover band known as The Pitts. With regular gigs in downtown St. Louis, I had a steady income, free beer and a good following. Occasionally, after-show parties followed the gigs, but only when we "sounded good." The Pitts' sound man, Zoo-Breath, was an over-the-road truck driver and a sound reinforcement novice. He always let me plug my mic into the "hot" channel of our 24 x 4 Kelsey mixer. The monitors were never loud enough, but after a few beers that never seemed to matter much.

Although I was on stage and got to make great eye contact with the crowd, I envied Zooie. He sat behind the console in control of everything. He even built and operated the lighting system. He used it at every gig although it made the PA buzz tremendously.

After college, I went to work as the Training Director for St. Louis Music, Inc. My job was to educate music retailers about the function and proper use of SLM's Ampeg and Crate amplification and Audio Centron sound reinforcement products. As I began to coordinate the first training program, I worked with SLM Electronics' design engineers. For the first time I understood why equipment has various knobs, controls and patching facilities. The engineers were different from the weekend warriors I gigged with; they used proper cables, matched levels, and actually considered impedance to improve sound.

The need to devise a succinct and casual way to communicate proper sound reinforcement theories, methods and applications to retailers became obvious. Proper equipment demoing would surely improve product performance and increase sales. Correcting the common mistakes made by bands like The Pitts (and many more "professional" bands) would help their sound and lengthen product life.

For over 10 years I have taught design and specification-oriented sound reinforcement theory and operation to people of all skill levels. While intrigued by all the wonderful new sound reinforcement products introduced each year, the lack of knowledge perpetuated by bands, institutions, churches, and music store personnel still amazes me.

There are wonderful publications available to help people improve the art and science of sound reinforcement. Unfortunately, many assume a certain level of reader proficiency that may or may not exist. It is intent of Sound Check to begin the reader at square one and explain the rudiments of professional PA in unison with more advanced information.

Regardless of your experience with sound reinforcement, I'm sure that Sound Check will increase your awareness, improve your understanding, and ultimately your sound.

The Nature of Sound

SOUND PROCESSES

"If a tree fell in the forest and no one was there to hear it, would it make a sound...?"

So goes the age old question to which there has never been a definitive answer. Until now, that is, because in its most complete definition, sound must have three essential elements; *generation*, *propagation* (or transmission) and *reception*.

So, if the tree fell and no one was there to hear it, the third essential element, reception, was missing, and therefore no sound occurred. All three elements are important, and an understanding of each is essential to a complete understanding of music and sound amplification.

In order for sound to be generated, something must set air in motion. This means that anything which vibrates can generate sound, whether it is the strings on a guitar, the reed in an oboe, or our own vocal cords.

The movement of any vibrating sound source can be characterized by the following criteria:

1. The motion takes place symmetrically about an equilibrium position. Translation: A pendulum when at rest will hang straight. This is equilibrium. As the pendulum is disturbed, it swings to the left and right of the equilibrium point. Another way to say this is the pendulum goes positive and negative in relation to equilibrium. **Fig. 1-1**

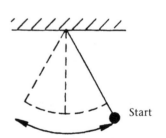

Figure 1-1

Start

2. Regardless of how far the source vibrates from equilibrium, the number of completed movements will remain the same. Translation: If two pendulums were the same length and pendulum A was pulled one foot while pendulum B was pulled five feet, both pendulums would cross equilibrium at the same time. **Fig. 1-2**

Figure 1-2

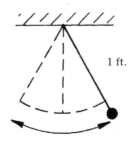
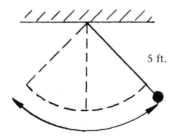

1 ft.

5 ft.

3.   The speed of the vibrating source will vary throughout the movement because of the force acting upon it and the inertial property of itself. Translation: As the pendulum swings toward its maximum positive or negative position, it will slow and eventually stop in order for it to return in the opposite direction. **Fig. 1-3**

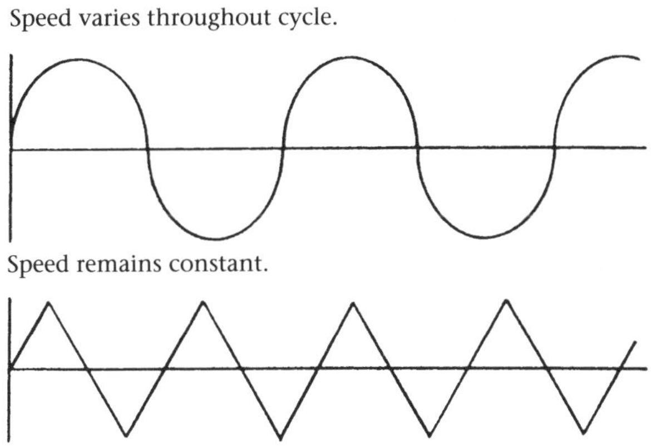

Speed varies throughout cycle.

Figure 1-3

Speed remains constant.

Consider a long tube that is open at one end and has a piston in the other. Attached to the piston is a tuning fork. The air in the tube is at normal atmospheric pressure which means all the air particles are evenly spaced and at rest. **Fig. 1-4**

As the tuning fork starts to vibrate, it pushes the piston at the same rate. Let's say the tuning fork vibrates one inch in either direction. As the tuning fork pushes the piston into the tube one inch, air particles are compressed one inch. The tuning fork then draws the piston back out to its original position. The air next to the piston now returns to equilibrium or normal atmospheric pressure. The compressed air is now two inches from the piston. As the tuning fork continues to vibrate, it pulls the piston backwards one inch, which creates a one inch area of air that is less than normal atmospheric pressure. This area where the air particles become more rare is known as rarefaction. Finally, the tuning fork returns to the original position where another one inch patch of air returns to equilibrium.

Figure 1-4

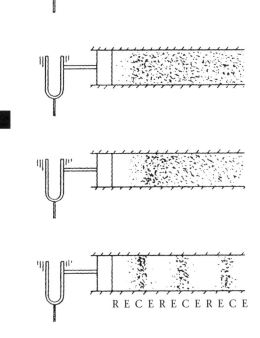

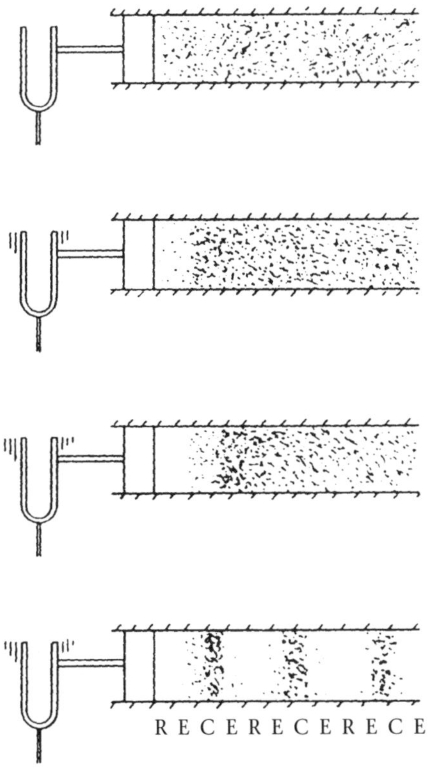

R E C E R E C E R E C E

One complete movement of the tuning fork (or any sound source) is known as a *cycle*. The air in the cylinder can be broken down into four areas: equilibrium to compression, compression back to equilibrium, equilibrium to rarefaction, and rarefaction back to equilibrium. This completed movement creates a cycle.

In this example, we illustrated movement but only in one direction. It is important to note, however, that sound travels in all directions. If a pebble is dropped into a pool of water, waves would spread outward from the point of the pebble's entry. **Fig. 1-5**

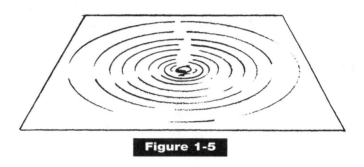

Figure 1-5

WAVEFORM CHARACTERISTICS
The Sine Wave

With all of this in mind, we can plot a graph for sound waves and/or sound sources. Suppose we dipped a pendulum in ink and started swinging it against a roll of paper moving perpendicularly to the direction of the swing. We would see that the paper would form a wave that looked like this: **Fig. 1-6**

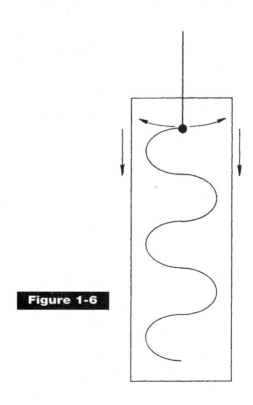

Figure 1-6

Now, turning the paper horizontally and drawing a line through the center of the wave would yield: **Fig. 1-7**

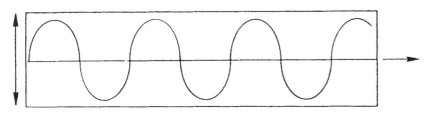

Figure 1-7

This wave form is known as a Sine Wave named after the trigonometric function. The horizontal line would represent time and the vertical line would represent the positive and negative (forward and backward) extents of the pendulum's movement. The time line would be referenced in seconds, milliseconds (1/1,000 second), or microseconds (1/1,000,000 second), and the extent line could be referenced with any distance measurement (inches, millimeters) or power measurement to achieve that distance (watts, volts, pounds, decibels, RPM's, etc.).

Frequency

A cycle can be defined as a completed movement of a wave before it repeats itself (remember the air in the tube). We can also plot time points of the cycle on our horizontal axis. In the example, **Fig. 1-8**, there is one complete cycle in one second known as one cycle per second or one CPS. Another term more commonly used for cycle per second is Hertz (abbreviated Hz). Hertz refers to how often the sound source vibrates in a one second interval. For example, an A440 tuning fork vibrates at 440 Hz which means it moves back and forth at a rate of 440 times per second.

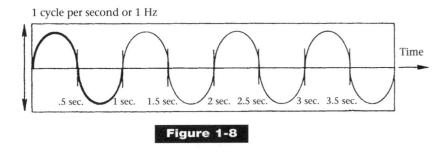

1 cycle per second or 1 Hz

Time

.5 sec.   1 sec.   1.5 sec.   2 sec.   2.5 sec.   3 sec.   3.5 sec.

Figure 1-8

Therefore, this rate measures the frequency of the movement, or how often it repeats in a one second interval. We use frequency to describe and determine pitch in sound. The greater the frequency (the more cycles per second), the higher the pitch we hear. 440 Hz is a lower pitched note than 880 Hz. Since the strings on a violin vibrate faster than the strings on a bass guitar, the bass guitar plays lower pitched notes.

Amplitude

The distance or extent of the wave from the equilibrium position is known as the amplitude of the wave. Here we have two waves with the same frequency (five cycles per second). The only difference between them is their differences in amplitude. Wave A has greater amplitude than Wave B. Amplitude refers to the intensity or loudness. **Fig. 1-9**

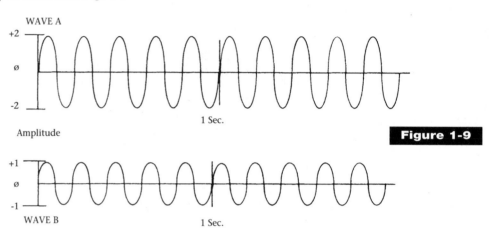

Figure 1-9

Phase

When two waveforms occur at the same time, they interact with one another and create a new wave form. Phase refers to the effect one wave has on another. Two waves which are started simultaneously having the same amplitude and frequency will produce a new wave with the same frequency but greater amplitude. **Fig. 1-10** In fact, the amplitude will be the sum of the amplitudes of each wave. These two waves are said to be *in phase*. The result would be a louder sound than either wave by itself.

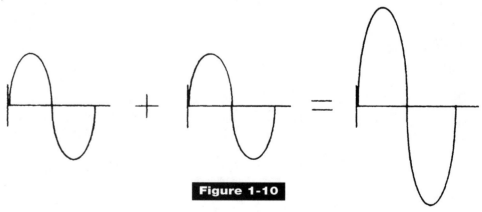

Figure 1-10

If two waves with the same amplitude and frequency are started with Wave A moving one direction (positive) and Wave B moving the opposite direction (negative), the waves would then cancel each other out and no sound would occur. **Fig 1-11** This is known as phase cancellation.

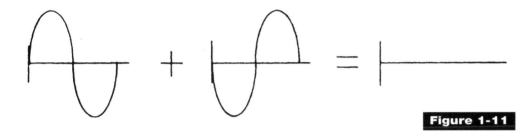

Figure 1-11

It can be seen that two waves having different frequencies and amplitudes can create a new, more complex wave. Here are a few examples. **Fig 1-12**

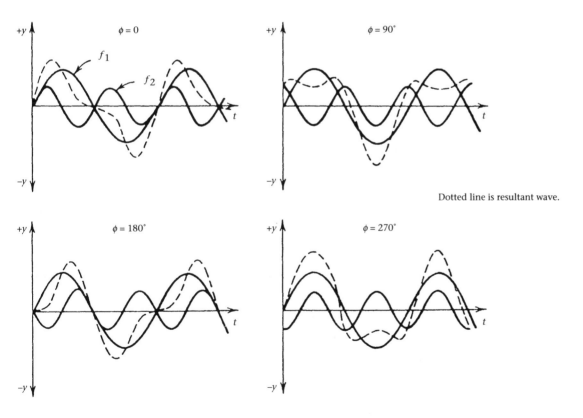

Dotted line is resultant wave.

Figure 1-12

Harmonics

A complex tone can be characterized as two or more waves having different frequencies, amplitudes, and phase relationships. Waves that have frequencies related by whole numbers are called harmonics. These harmonics can be added to pure tones by electronic means or can be inherent in the instrument itself.

If the same note was played on a piano and a violin, it would be easy to differentiate the two instruments. The reason a piano sounds different from a violin is because of the different harmonics that are naturally generated by the two instruments. To put it another way, harmonics are "ghost" tones that are generated as a result of the structure or playing method of the instrument.

For example, when an A440 tone is played on a piano, the piano string vibrates at 440 Hz which is called the fundamental. However, other vibrations occur as well because of the structure of the piano. Those notes would be two times the fundamental, three times the fundamental, four times the fundamental, etc. This means although we perceive the pitch of 440 Hz, other pitches like 880 Hz, 1320 Hz, 1760 Hz, etc. are also present and they affect the overall tone of the piano. The amount of harmonics and the intensity of each in relation to the fundamental create a distinctive sound unique to each instrument. This is known as the timbre of the instrument. **Fig. 1-13**

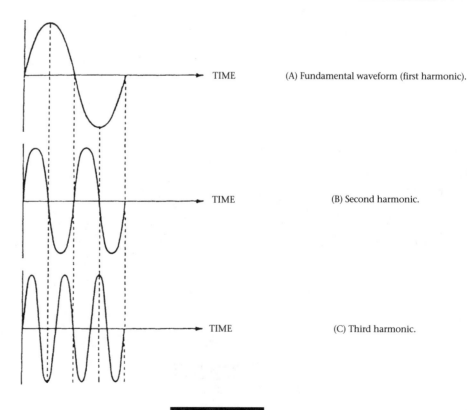

(A) Fundamental waveform (first harmonic).

(B) Second harmonic.

(C) Third harmonic.

Figure 1-13A

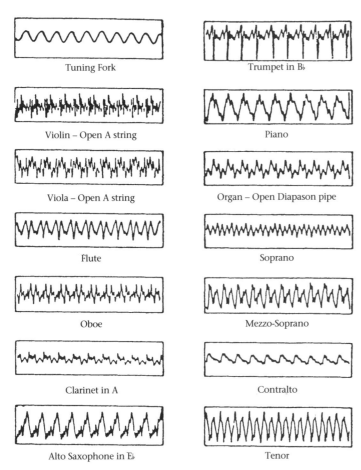

Tuning Fork

Trumpet in B♭

Violin – Open A string

Piano

Viola – Open A string

Organ – Open Diapason pipe

Flute

Soprano

Oboe

Mezzo-Soprano

Clarinet in A

Contralto

Alto Saxophone in E♭

Tenor

Figure 1-13B

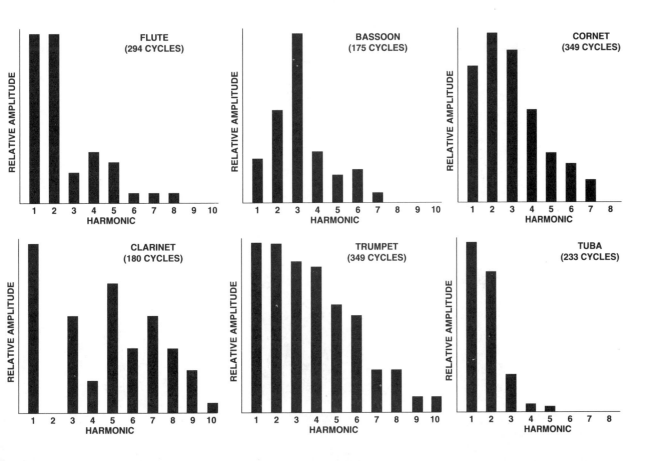

FLUTE
(294 CYCLES)

BASSOON
(175 CYCLES)

CORNET
(349 CYCLES)

Figure 1-13C

CLARINET
(180 CYCLES)

TRUMPET
(349 CYCLES)

TUBA
(233 CYCLES)

Reception of Sound

The reception and perception of sound is a combination of physical and psychological attributes. Barring any physical deficiency, we are all anatomically capable of hearing. Our ears receive complex waveforms and our brain deciphers them. But psychological factors are what determine whether something sounds "good" or not.

ANATOMICAL STRUCTURE OF THE EAR

The ear is divided into three parts: outer, middle, and inner ear. **Fig. 2-1**

The outer ear consists of the external part (pinna), an auditory canal which leads to a membrane at the end called the eardrum.

The middle ear is the section just after the eardrum. It consists of three bones called the ossicles, individually named the hammer, anvil, and the stirrup. From the throat, the Eustachian tube connects here to permit equal pressure to be maintained on each side of the eardrum. That is why as air pressure changes, as on an airplane, our ears "pop" and yawning helps regain equilibrium.

The inner ear has two holes, the oval and the round window, on a liquid filled, coiled cavity called the cochlea. **Fig. 2-2** Dividing this cavity lengthwise is the basilar membrane. Hair-like cells along this membrane become activated to perceive sound.

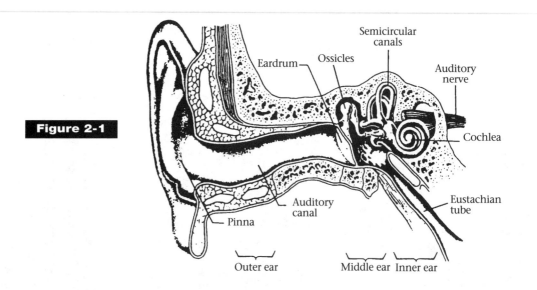

Figure 2-1

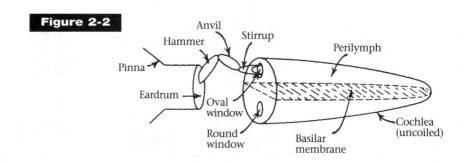

Figure 2-2

HOW THE EAR WORKS

Sound waves travel through the auditory canal pushing and rarefying against the eardrum. The drum vibrates and moves the ossicles. Vibrations travel to the Inner Ear through the round window disturbing the fluid in the cochlea. The basilar membrane is set into motion by the fluid and the hair cells pickup this motion. These hair cells initiate impulses to the nervous system and sound is perceived in the brain. Pure tones activate only a few hairs on a particular portion of the basilar membrane. As frequency changes, different sections of the basilar are activated. Higher frequencies activate hair cells nearer the round window while lower frequencies activate the opposite end.

FREQUENCY AS PITCH

Pitch and frequency are closely related. Pitch is one of the most obvious psychological attributes of musical sound, while frequency is a physical phenomenon. We perceive pitch from the frequency of a wave. We will mention pitch and frequency in an interchangeable manner and will bypass the physiological, neurological, and psychological elements that are associated with pitch. We will refer to pitch and frequency in Hertz.

Our ears can detect pitches from 20 Hz to 20,000 Hz. We do not hear all these frequencies equally however. We are more sensitive to mid-range frequencies than we are to low and high frequencies. This unequal sensitivity to frequencies also changes with levels. At low volumes, we do not hear low frequencies well at all. However, as listening levels increase, we tend to hear those frequencies at a more equal level to the mids. **Fig. 2-3**

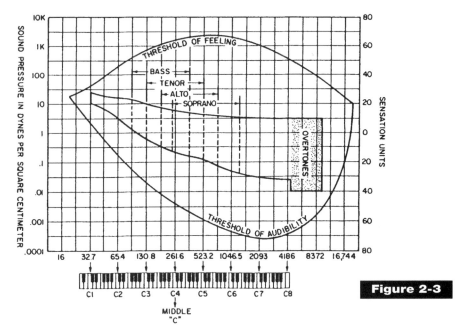

Figure 2-3

This is because as listening levels increase, the bones in our middle ear vibrate along with the ear drum increasing the perceived sound level. At low volumes, these bones do not vibrate and hence we do not hear the low frequencies as well. This is the concept of a loudness button on a stereo which, in part, increases the level of lows when you listen at low volumes.

INTENSITY OF SOUND WAVES

A source which vibrates the air is really transferring energy into that medium. This energy propagates through the air in the form of sound. Put another way, the sound source radiates acoustical energy . **Fig. 2-4**

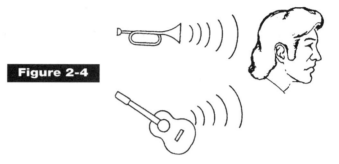

Figure 2-4

Musical instruments radiate this acoustical energy and the rate at which an instrument radiates that energy is that instrument's "power output". Our ears are sensitive to this acoustic power. The measurement for this acoustic power is the *acoustic watt.*

The human ear is quite a remarkable tool. It has the unique ability to detect very quiet and very loud sounds. If a sound source had the ability to generate one acoustic watt of power, it would be perceived as being very loud. In fact, it would hurt our ears. This is known as the "threshold of pain."

Remarkably, if a sound source produced a sound of only one trillionth of one acoustic watt (.000000000001 acoustic watts), we would still be able to hear it. This sound would be very soft and is called the "threshold of sound." Therefore, the difference between the loudest sound we can tolerate is one trillion times greater than the slightest sound we can hear.

Because of this wide range of hearing, using the unit acoustic watt would be difficult because of the large numbers involved. So, instead of using acoustic power and acoustic watts, we will use *Sound Pressure Level* and measure it in *Decibels.*

Another important fact about hearing is that it is non-linear. That is, doubling the acoustic power of an instrument will not be doubling the loudness. The decibel scale of measurement takes the non-linear nature of hearing into account, so it is a more descriptive measure of how we actually hear.

Decibels (abbreviated dB) are based on ratios and logarithms. Don't let these terms frighten you. Logarithms are simply a way to reduce large ranges of numbers. We said that the range of human hearing is from .000000000001 acoustic watt to one acoustic watt. Using decibels we can replace those numbers with zero decibels as the slightest sound we can hear up to 120 dB for the loudest sound. So **Fig. 2-5A** can be replaced with **Fig. 2-5B**.

The decibel system can be used to measure practically anything because it is based on ratios. It is always comparing one level to another. We cannot say a car's top speed is 50 decibels, but we can say that Car A is 10 dB faster than Car B. (Zero dB has to be referenced to something like MPH).

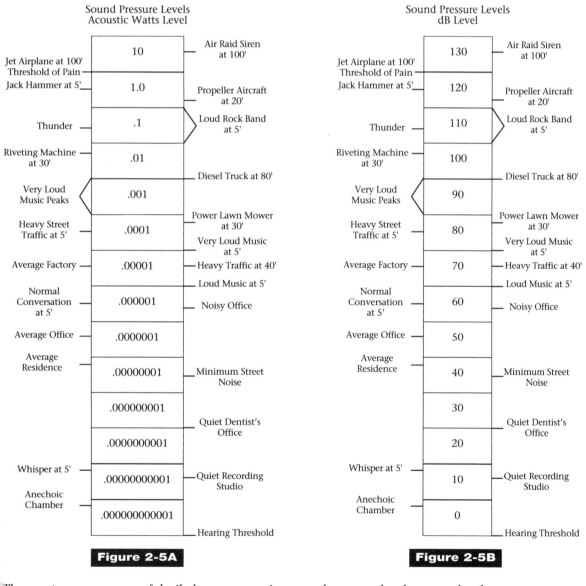

Figure 2-5A

Figure 2-5B

The most common uses of decibels are comparing sound pressure levels, power levels, and voltage levels. It's important to remember that there has to be some comparative number. For example, zero dB SPL is the slightest sound that we can hear. To say a concert is 90 decibels means that the sound pressure level at the concert is 90 dB greater than the slightest sound we can hear or 30 dB less than pain.

More will be said on decibels throughout this guide. For now, the important points of decibels include power and sound pressure level relationships. The following table shows the relationship for various numbers. **Fig. 2-6**

Change of dB	Change of Power
0	1
1	1.3
2	1.6
3	2
4	2.5
5	3.2
6	4
7	5
8	6
9	8
10	10
11	12
12	16
15	32
18	64
20	100
30	1,000
40	10,000
50	100,000
60	1,000,000
70	10,000,000
80	100,000,000
90	1,000,000,000
100	10,000,000,000
110	100,000,000,000
120	1,000,000,000,000

Figure 2-6

This chart shows how more power is required to attain a particular dB increase. For example, if you want to increase SPL (sound pressure level) by 10 dB, you need to increase the power by ten times the existing amount. Let's say you were using a 100 watt amplifier which produced an SPL level of 95 dB. In order to get to 105 dB SPL, you would need a 1000 watt amplifier (10 times 100 watts).

Decibels are used for describing sound pressure levels because of their similarity to how humans hear. There are three rules to remember:

1. A one decibel change in sound pressure is impossible for most people to detect.

2. The average human hears loudness differences at 3 dB increments. This means in order to generate a *slight change in perceived loudness, power must be doubled.*

3. In order *to double the perceived loudness*, sound pressure level must be increased by *10 dB*, which *requires 10 times the power*!

So, if you had a 60 watt guitar amplifier, in order to make the sound just one increment louder (3 dB), you would need a 120 watt amplifier (60 times two). In order to be twice as loud, you would need a 600 watt amplifier (60 times ten).

Basic Electricity

In order to obtain a better appreciation of electronic musical instruments, we need to have a basic understanding of electricity and its components. Those components include voltage, current, resistance, and power. All of these interact and by using simple definitions and examples, we can see these interrelationships. While these examples show the fundamental workings of electricity, it is important to point out that electricity is a unique phenomenon and no analogy is perfect.

VOLTAGE

Voltage is commonly referred to as electrical pressure, and can also be thought of as electrical *intensity*.

Voltage is similar to the pressure of water which is stored in a dam. Measured at the base, the water has tremendous pressure, regardless of whether or not it is flowing. The taller the dam, the greater the pressure at the base. The higher that pressure is, the more powerful the flow when the water is released. Voltage is the potential for current in the same way water pressure is the potential for flow. In the case of voltage, what is being stored behind the dam is electrons, and high voltage is similar to a tall dam.

Voltage is that force which causes current to flow through an electronic circuit. Two common sources of voltage are batteries and the electrical outlets in your house. Most household electrical outlets have an electrical pressure or *potential* of 117 volts.

CURRENT

All substances are made up of atoms and each atom consists of tiny particles called electrons. These electrons in some atoms are very stable while in other materials they are very unstable. Electrons in less stable atoms can be made to "jump" from one atom to another. Materials that will "give up" electrons easily in this manner are known as conductors. This movement of electrons is called current flow. This flow of current is rated in *Amperes* (or Amps). Examples of conductors include copper, aluminum, and other metals. **Fig. 3-1**

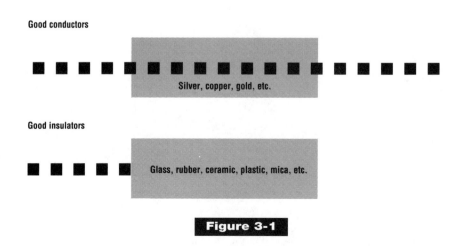

Good conductors

Silver, copper, gold, etc.

Good insulators

Glass, rubber, ceramic, plastic, mica, etc.

Figure 3-1

Most non-metals are poor conductors and are known as insulators. These include rubber and plastic. Certain insulators are used to cover conductors (such as copper wire) for protection and to channel the current properly.

Types of Current

There are two types of current flow: direct current (DC) and alternating current (AC).

Fig. 3-2

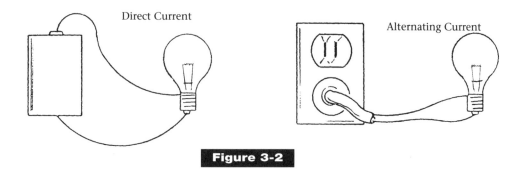

Figure 3-2

Direct current means the flow of electrons is in one direction: from negative to positive. Batteries are the most common type of DC source. Like the difference in height between the top and bottom of the dam, there is an excess of electrons within the *minus* portion of the battery which is expressed as voltage (AA batteries are 1.5V). Connecting a wire or some other conductor between the positive and negative nodes on the battery results in a flow of current from the negative (–) to the positive (+), until the excess of electrons is depleted.

The other type of current is *alternating current*. This is the current available in your houses. Alternating current changes directions at regular intervals. House current is 60 cycles which means the current at the two prongs of an AC outlet changes from positive to negative 60 times per second. The way in which current changes direction can be observed on an oscilloscope: the familiar sine wave. In fact "60 cycle hum" is the sound of AC current which has "leaked" into a sound system.

This highlights up an important connection between the alternation of current inherent in AC (from positive to negative back to positive) and the alternation of pressure in the production of sound (from compression to rarefaction back to compression). Audio signals travel using alternating current.

RESISTANCE

Electrical resistance is the name given to the internal friction involved in the passage of electrons through a wire, or through any material. In order for us to use electricity, we must be able to control the flow of current. This is done with resistance.

Using water as an example, turning a faucet handle is like changing the resistance to the flow of water. Even with the faucet in the wide open position, however, there is still resistance due to the friction of the water within the pipe.

Good conductors offer very little resistance, while good insulators have high resistance. The degree of resistance is measured in ohms, often designated with the Ω symbol. Another term used for resistance is impedance, also expressed in ohms. A speaker is a type of resistor, which is why one of the ways a speaker is described is in ohms (typically 32Ω, 16Ω, 8Ω or 4Ω).

Not too surprisingly, the rate at which current can flow is related (directly proportional) to the amount of resistance placed in opposition to that flow.

POWER

In everyday terms, people use the word power to mean a variety of things. In technical terms, power means *how fast work is done*, or *how fast energy is transferred*.

For example, if an elevator lifts 500 pounds 150 feet, and it takes 15 seconds to do it, the power is 5,000 (500 x 150 / 15) foot-pounds/second. Notice that this is expressed as a rate: how much work is done *in a given amount of time*. **One horsepower** is similarly expressed as a rate of energy expended: 550 ft.-lb./sec. The elevator in our example is doing work at the rate of 9.1 horsepower (5000/550).

If you imagine a dam, the work that the water can do turning a generator during a given period of time depends upon both the water's pressure and the size of the opening (size of the flow). Thinking of the water pressure at the dam's opening as its voltage, and the water rushing through the opening as the current, you can see that the power is the pressure times the size of the flow. Since the unit of measurement for electrical power is the Watt (designated with the letter P), our formula in electrical terms is **watts = voltage x current**, or:

$$P = E \times I$$

Wattage is simply the measurement of the rate of energy expended. For example, 746 Watts equals one Horsepower.

OHM'S LAW

In numeric terms, the potential power or **Voltage** (expressed in Volts, V, or as E in formulas) **divided by the resistance** (expressed in ohms, Ω, or as R in formulas) **is equal to the Amperage** or current (expressed in Amps, A, or as I in formulas).

The set of mathematical relationships which tie together the various characteristics of electricity is known as Ohm's Law. They are presented here in the form of equation diagrams. To solve the equations, place your finger over the unknown variable and perform the remaining equation. For example, in the first chart, placing your finger over E (solving voltage), you would then multiply I x R; or placing your finger over I (solving current), you would then divide E by R. **Fig. 3-3**

Figure 3-3

CURRENT FLOW PROPOERTIES

There are two primary properties of current. The first is heat. This is caused by the flow of current through wire (a conductor). Because of the excitement of electrons, the wire becomes hot and if enough current is present may begin to glow. This property is used in toasters, electric heaters, and light bulbs.

Another property of current is electromagnetism. When current flows through a coil of wire, the coil acts like a magnet. This is because a magnetic field is created around the wire. Any magnetic metal or material passed through this field will also become "charged" and will take on the properties of a magnet. **Fig. 3-4**

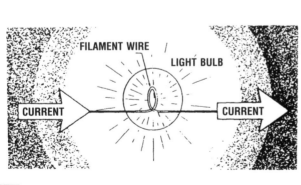 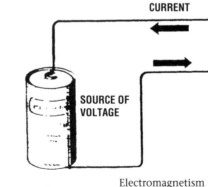

Figure 3-4   Heat   Electromagnetism

A simple experiment demonstrating this property consists of wrapping a wire around a nail and attaching the two ends of the wire to a battery. The nail becomes magnetized and can be used to pick up metal filings.

In music and sound reinforcement, the property of electromagnetism is used in electric guitar pickups, microphones, and speakers.

Loudspeakers and Speaker Enclosures

A loudspeaker is a transducer which means it takes one kind of energy and converts it to another. A speaker converts electrical energy into acoustical energy. Let's take a closer look at the basic operation of any loudspeaker. A speaker uses the principles of magnetism. A magnet has two opposite forces contained in itself, generally called north and south poles (also called positive and negative). Unlike poles attract while like poles oppose each other. **Fig. 4-1**

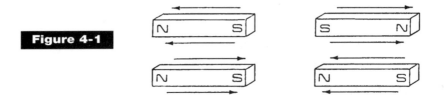

Figure 4-1

Speakers use a fixed, permanent magnet and a moveable electromagnet. The electro-magnet is created by current flowing through a coil of wire. The current traveling to the coil is AC (alternating current), and it changes its direction according to the frequency of the signal (the sound being amplified). As the current passes through the coil in one direction, it creates positive magnetic field. Two magnetic fields repel each other, so the coil begins to move out, away from the magnet. When the signal changes direction, the coil is forced to move in the opposite direction. **Fig. 4-2**

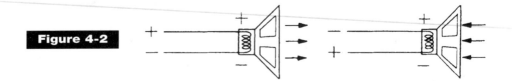

Figure 4-2

If a pure note, say 440 Hz, is played through the amplifier, the current goes through a positive/negative cycle 440 times per second, moving the coil back and forth accordingly. The coil is attached to a paper cone, and as the coil moves the cone moves with it in a pumping motion. The forward pumping action of the cone compresses the air. As it begins its motion backward it pulls the air through equilibrium to rarefaction, repeating the complete cycle 440 times a second, very closely matching the sound of our A440 tuning fork.

The operation and efficiency of a speaker depend upon the combination of the parts used. Let's take a closer look at the parts that make up a speaker. **Fig. 4-3**

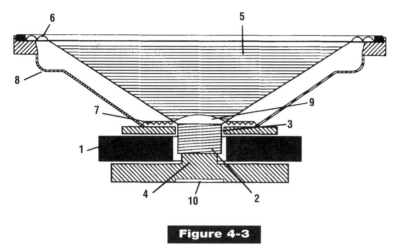

Figure 4-3

1. **Magnet** - The magnet size determines how strong a magnetic field can be generated. Within certain limits, the larger the magnet, the more efficient the speaker usually is because of more control over the voice coil and greater dissipation of heat. It also means more weight and expense. In fact, the magnet assembly is usually the single most expensive component of a speaker.

2. **Voice Coil** - The voice coil is wire windings around a cylinder (called a voice coil former or bobbin), often made of plastic, aluminum, paper, or fiberglass. Since this coil of wire is continuously handling high amounts of current from the amplifier during operation, high power-handling speakers must incorporate materials in the former to add heat sinking and/or mechanical integrity. The voice coil former should have sufficient strength and temperature resistance to maintain concentricity (roundness). The wire can be made of aluminum or copper, and is either round wound or flat wound. Aluminum is lightweight (moves easily) but copper is a better conductor of electricity (less power loss). Flat wound wire allows closer tolerance and greater wire density in the gap which helps efficiency.

3. **Gap** - The gap is the space in the magnet assembly for the voice coil to move in. This is where the area of the electromagnetic field is focused. By narrowing the gap, efficiency is increased because of greater magnetic field interaction and the tight proximity allows more heat dissipation into the magnet. If the gap is very close, the suspension must be very accurate because if the coil touches something in the magnet assembly, the speaker will short out or begin to rub.

4. **Pole Piece and Plates** - The pole piece is sandwiched between the front and rear plates. These metal pieces become magnetized and direct the magnetic field so it is concentrated into the gap. It also transfers heat into the magnet.

5.   **Cone** - The cone, made of paper or synthetic material, is glued to the voice coil and is used to actually disturb or push the air. The shape of the cone, either straight or curvilinear, affects the frequency response (curvilinear provides greater high frequency) and also affects the rigidity of the cone (a straight cone maintains shape better). The cone can also contain ribs which add stiffness but because they use thicker paper, are more difficult to move.

6.   **Surround** - The surround or compliance connects the cone to the speaker basket helping the speaker maintain its round shape, as well as determining how far out the speaker may travel. It may be made from polyurethane foam, cloth, or paper, and may have rolls or pleats allowing stiffness or long travel.

7.   **Spider** - The spider connects the voice coil former or the beginning of the cone to the basket to center the voice coil in the gap. It, like the surround, has rolls or pleats to allow the pumping action of the speaker and prevent excessive excursions.

8.   **Basket** - The basket is the framework for all the speaker's components. Different types such as stamped metal versus die cast offer strength and durability. Cast should be used when larger magnets need to be supported. Some proponents of die cast aluminum baskets argue that it aids in heat sinking and does not interfere with the magnetic field, making it more efficient.

9.   **Dust Cap** - The dust cap merely protects the voice coil and gap area from dirt. It can be made from aluminum, paper, or cloth. If an aluminum dust cap is used and connected to the voice coil, it can aid in reproducing higher frequencies.

10. **Vent** - Many premium speakers have an opening in the back of the magnet assembly called the vent to allow additional cooling of the gap area. It's primary function is to relieve the pressure built up under the dust cap caused by coil motion.

DRIVER TYPES

Speakers can generally be categorized as producers and reproducers. Reproducers try to recreate the sound of the signal very accurately, like speakers for home stereos and sound reinforcement. A perfect reproducing speaker would be able to reproduce all frequencies equally from 20 Hz–20 kHz. This could be plotted on a graph called a frequency response curve which looks like the following. **Fig. 4-4**

Figure 4-4

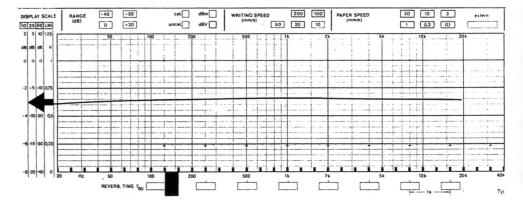

In actuality, it is impossible for a single speaker to produce a perfectly even frequency response because of the different combinations of materials used in its construction. Speaker sizes can also affect the tonal characteristics of a loudspeaker. Cone speakers come in a variety of sizes from 32" to as small as 1". Larger diameter speakers tend to reproduce low frequencies better than high frequencies, while smaller diameter speakers cannot recreate low frequencies.

Musical instrument amplifiers such as guitar and bass amps use speakers that have tonal characteristics which accentuate the frequency response of the instrument creating a new, unique timbre. These special tonal characteristics result from the selection of the shape and material of the cone, the voice coil size, type, and material, suspension types and materials, and other construction considerations.

Below are examples of frequency responses for different guitar amp speakers. Note the coloration of the signal and how it enhances certain frequency ranges while de-emphasizing others. **Fig. 4-5**

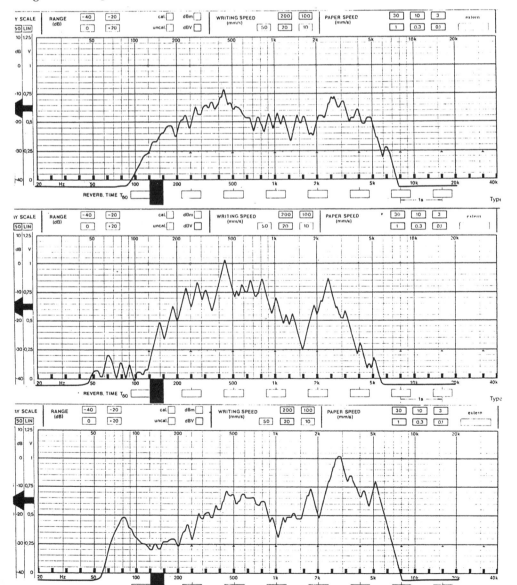

Figure 4-5

Reproducing speakers are made to have smooth frequency responses throughout their effective range. In order to have wide frequency response, speaker cabinets use several different sized components. This is usually accomplished by combining cone loudspeakers with differing diameters like a 15" speaker for low frequencies, 10" speaker for mid range, and a 3" speaker for highs. This is done quite often in the home stereo speakers.

Besides cone loudspeakers, there are other types of "drivers" used to generate sound other than the conventional cone loudspeaker. One such device is a compression driver. A compression driver uses the same design approach in that there is a diaphragm attached to a voice coil centered within a fixed magnet. The differences are the shape of the driver and the diaphragm is larger than the opening of the sound chamber. This throat area allows more pressure to be built up, creating greater efficiency in the driver.

Fig. 4-6

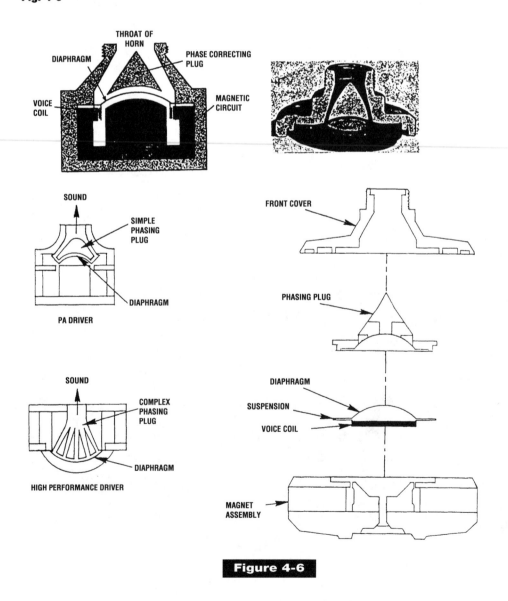

Figure 4-6

In front of the diaphragm is a bullet-shaped device called a phase plug. The phase plug equalizes the distance from all points of the diaphragm to the throat of the driver. This prevents any phase cancellation and ensures smooth frequency response. **Fig. 4-7**

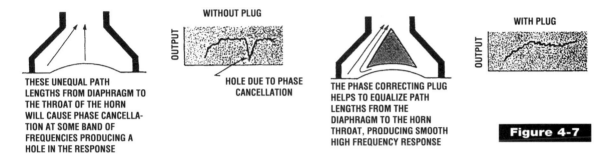

WITHOUT PLUG

OUTPUT

THESE UNEQUAL PATH LENGTHS FROM DIAPHRAGM TO THE THROAT OF THE HORN WILL CAUSE PHASE CANCELLATION AT SOME BAND OF FREQUENCIES PRODUCING A HOLE IN THE RESPONSE

HOLE DUE TO PHASE CANCELLATION

THE PHASE CORRECTING PLUG HELPS TO EQUALIZE PATH LENGTHS FROM THE DIAPHRAGM TO THE HORN THROAT, PRODUCING SMOOTH HIGH FREQUENCY RESPONSE

WITH PLUG

OUTPUT

Figure 4-7

Compression drivers are generally more efficient than their cone driver counterparts. Cone loudspeakers' efficiency varies from one to ten percent, depending on the design. This means that from one to ten percent of the energy sent to the speaker will be converted to sound. The rest will be dissipated in the form of heat. Compression drivers coupled to horns can have efficiency ratings upwards of 20–30%.

Piezo tweeters are another type of driver which utilizes a crystal. When pressure is applied to a crystal, electrical polarization takes place and current is generated. The current is proportional to the mechanical strain placed upon the crystal. The inverse of this effect is present when current is applied to the crystal. As current is applied, the crystal will begin to vibrate proportional to the current.

A piezo tweeter uses a crystal attached to a small diaphragm or cone. As the crystal vibrates, the diaphragm moves and sound is created. Because of the small size of the diaphragm and limited movement of the crystal, a piezo tweeter is used for high frequency reproduction only.

CROSSOVERS

The best approach to making a full range speaker enclosure is to use a device called a crossover, which allows a certain frequency range to be sent to a specific driver. There are two types of crossovers commonly used. A passive or high level crossover and an active or electronic crossover.

A passive crossover uses the same principles as tone controls. A capacitor is an electronic device which allows high frequencies to pass but blocks low frequencies. An inductor, usually a coil of wire, blocks high frequencies but allows low frequencies to pass. A crossover on a two-way speaker with a 15" cone driver for the lows and a compression driver for the highs would allow only high frequencies to be sent to the compression driver and the lows to the 15" speaker.

Passive crossovers are often called high level crossovers because they take the high current level from a power amp and then split the frequency ranges. Care must be taken in designing the crossover so it can handle the high power signal levels sent from the power amplifier. The crossover frequency is predetermined by the manufacturer.

Fig. 4-8

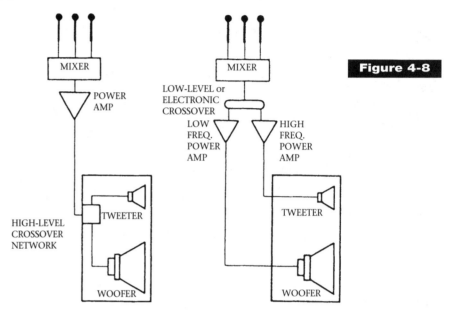

Figure 4-8

Electronic crossovers are used before the power amps. They take full range signals of low voltage levels and split them into separate frequency ranges. Each frequency range can then be amplified by a separate power amp and then sent to the appropriate speaker component.

Because they operate at low voltage levels, electronic (active) crossovers are generally more efficient than passive crossovers. Electronic crossovers usually have individual controls to adjust the levels of the lows and highs. They also offer the advantage of allowing the user to select a desired crossover point. **Fig. 4-9**

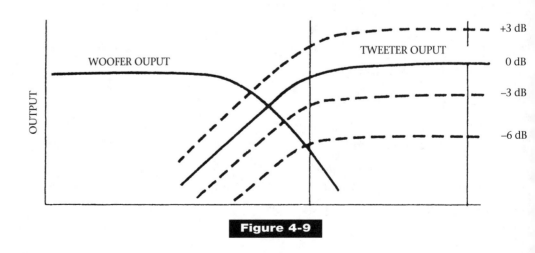

Figure 4-9

The number of different components used will determine the number of crossover points needed. A two-way system will require one, a three-way system will need two, a four-way system three, and so on. Many electronic crossovers come in two-way, three-way, four-way, or even five-way configurations. However, each frequency range requires its own power amp. This process in a two-way system is called bi-amping. In a three-way system it is called tri-amping, etc.

Regardless of the type of crossover used, the operation is the same. At the crossover frequency, signal level is reduced three to six dB. It is important to reduce levels at this point or both speaker components will be equally reproducing the same frequency. This would cause a peak at that frequency and prevent a smooth frequency response.

Fig. 4-10A

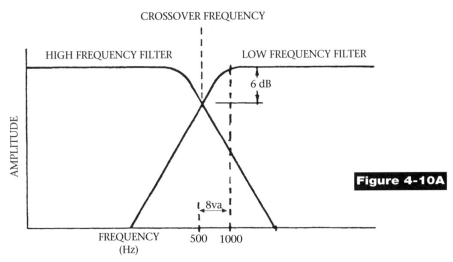

Signal levels in each frequency range will continue to be reduced at a given rate called a slope rate, rated in decibels per octave (dB/8va). (An octave is the doubling or halving of a frequency.) A crossover with a slope of six dB/8va would lower the signal level by a factor of six dB each octave.

Suppose we had a two-way speaker (15" cone driver and small compression driver) with a crossover point of 1,000 Hz. The signal going to the high frequency component would be reduced three dB at the crossover point (1,000 Hz). At one octave under 1,000 Hz (500 Hz), the signal would drop six more dB or a total of –9 dB from the average high frequency output. The next octave down (250 Hz) would be sent to the compression driver, but the signal level at that point would be reduced another six dB for a total of –15 dB.

The compression driver in this example can do a more efficient job reproducing high frequencies because it is not being forced to reproduce low frequencies as well. The crossover also protects and extends the life of the speaker components.

Different crossovers can have different slope rates. Twelve dB/8va, 18 dB/8va, and 24 dB/8va are commonly found in quality sound reinforcement systems. In general, the higher the slope rate, the better the protection to the speaker components. **Fig. 4-10B**

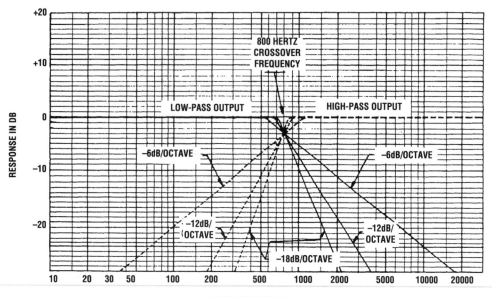

Figure 4-10B

SPEAKER ENCLOSURE TYPES

In order to understand speaker enclosures, we must first discuss the speaker baffle. Suspended by itself, a speaker would interfere with its own output. As the speaker cone moves, it pushes air from both the front and the rear. Because the rear wave produced is exactly opposite of the front wave, they are out of phase, the opposing air movements for the most part cancel each other out especially at low frequencies. The resulting sound is weak and tinny. **Fig. 4-11**

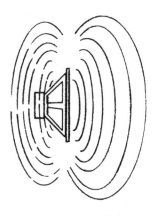

Figure 4-11

To prevent "phase cancellation", the front wave must be separated from the rear wave. This is accomplished by using a device called a baffle. A baffle can be defined as a device which routes the sound energy. There are many different baffle configurations labeled as direct radiators.

Direct Radiators

A direct radiator is a speaker which propagates sound directly into the listening area. There are no other acoustic elements between the speaker and the ear other than the air itself. By using a baffle, several benefits can be obtained. One is that because phase problems are eliminated, better low frequency response can be obtained. Another benefit is that the baffle actually adds to the radiating surface of the driver. That is not to say the baffle should vibrate, however. What this means is that as sound comes out of the enclosure, it hits the front baffle and bounces the sound energy into the listening area.

1. **Infinite Baffle** - If a speaker was mounted on a board of infinite length and width, the back wave would never meet with the front and no cancellation would occur. An example of this type of speaker cabinet would be to mount a speaker in a wall between two rooms. The sound from the front of the speaker would propagate into one room while the rear wave would project into the other. This would totally prevent any front to rear phase cancellations. The only problem is that this type of speaker would not be portable.

    To solve this problem, the speaker can be placed in a sealed box so there is no way for the rear wave to get out. No phase cancellation would occur. But because the rear wave gets compressed into the box, it acts like a spring pushing the cone forward. This makes the speaker very inefficient and reduces sound pressure level because half of the energy produced by the speaker is wasted. **Fig. 4-12**

2. **Finite Baffle** - The most obvious way to increase an infinite baffle cabinet's efficiency is to open up the back part of the cabinet. This allows the speaker to move freely, increasing its sound pressure level. **Fig. 4-13**

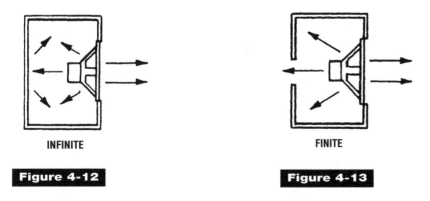

INFINITE   FINITE

Figure 4-12   **Figure 4-13**

However, depending upon the size of the baffle, a certain amount of phase cancellation will take place. This will be dependent upon the required frequency. For example, in order to reproduce a frequency of 50 Hz which has a wavelength of over 22 feet, the distance from the edge of the speaker to the edge of the baffle would have to be 5.5 feet. Of course, this baffle could be folded back like the sides of the enclosure. This is the type of cabinet commonly used with guitar amplifiers because it allows very high sound pressure levels. The frequencies affected by the phase cancellation here are below the guitar's frequencies anyway.

3. **Bass-Reflex** - All drivers have a certain frequency response and within that response is a peak at low frequencies known as the free-air resonance peak. **Fig. 4-14** This means when the speaker is asked to produce that frequency, it resonates and has greater amplitude at that frequency. After that point, the low frequencies taper off at a rapid rate. Different baffle designs can be used to eliminate the boominess caused by the resonant frequency.

    Recall that a problem with infinite baffle enclosures is that the rear wave is not radiated into the listening area, so 1/2 of the speaker's energy is wasted. We can utilize that rear wave by supplying a vent in which the rear wave of the speaker can be used. This is the principle behind a bass reflex enclosure. **Fig. 4-15**

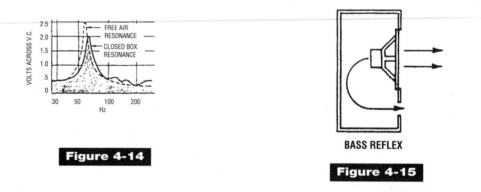

Figure 4-14

BASS REFLEX

Figure 4-15

There is a direct relationship between the size of the enclosure, the size of the port, and the resonant frequency of the driver. When these three factors are balanced correctly, the port will actually aid the speaker in reproducing low frequencies by creating more mass to allow the sound to pulse out. **Fig. 4-16**

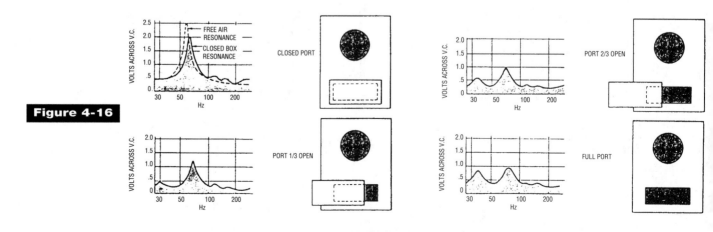

Figure 4-16

A properly designed bass reflex cabinet eliminates the large resonant peak and creates two smaller peaks at octaves above and below the free-air resonance point. In doing this, the low frequency response is actually extended and a smoother attenuation of lows is achieved.

Because the bass reflex cabinet must be "tuned", the size of the enclosure may have to be exceptionally large to obtain proper phase inversion. By using a vent with a duct, the enclosure volume can be greatly reduced while still maintaining proper tuning. There are several types of bass reflex cabinets. They include a ducted port, a shelved port, and an acoustical labyrinth.

Ducted port cabinets have a tube before the port hole in order to select the proper resonant frequency of the cabinet. **Fig. 4-17**

A shelved port has a "shelf" which extends back into the cabinet to allow the proper wave alignment, as well as a larger port area. **Fig. 4-18**

An acoustical labyrinth is a shelved, ported cabinet with an extra vertical extension creating a "maze" for the sound wave to travel through. This places more load on the rear surface of the speaker cushioning the sound and giving the cabinet a smooth, equal response. This tuning process is similar to pipe organ tuning. **Fig. 4-19**

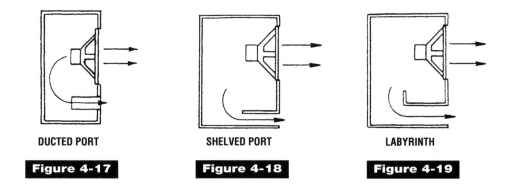

DUCTED PORT   SHELVED PORT   LABYRINTH

Figure 4-17   **Figure 4-18**   **Figure 4-19**

Horns

Horns are probably the oldest type of baffling dating back to the days of Edison and his phonograph. The expanding cone attached to the phonograph needle "amplified" the sound. In actuality, a horn is not an amplifier but an acoustical transformer. Because the pressure coming from a driver is high impedance versus the low impedance air, a great deal of power is required to reproduce sound. By its gradually increasing size, a horn transforms the high air pressure at the throat of the driver to low air pressure at the mouth of the horn. This allows a better impedance match to the low impedance of air. **Fig. 4-20**

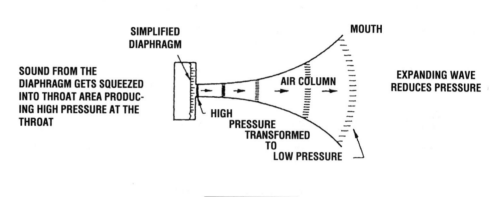

Figure 4-20

A horn actually increases efficiency of the driver by this impedance matching which means less power is required to the driver to achieve loudness. A cone speaker can have an efficiency rating of 1–10%, while a driver attached to a horn can be as much as 40% efficient.

Another benefit of a horn is the ability to extend low frequencies. Since low frequencies have large wavelengths, it is difficult for a driver with a small diaphragm to effectively move the large volume of air pressure needed for low frequencies. By using a horn, a diaphragm's small movements can couple these low frequencies to the air.

A driver diaphragm should be larger than the opening (throat) of the horn. This forces a lot of pressure into a smaller area and makes the driver more efficient. When this is done, there must be pressure applied to the rear of the driver or the speaker will move in more than it will move out. This can cause a type of distortion called non-linear distortion. That is, the speaker's movement is no longer symmetrical. Compression drivers have a rear compression chamber which equalizes the pressure of the diaphragm on both sides to prevent non-linear distortion. **Fig. 4-21**

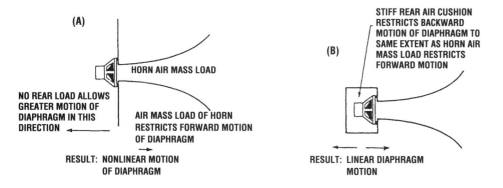

Figure 4-21

Horns can be used for woofers or tweeters but the reason for using a horn is to extend the frequency range of the driver and to attain a more concentrated dispersion of sound.

"Front" and "rear horn loading" refers to a process of combining horns and bass reflex with the same driver. This is done to achieve the advantages of both systems. A front loaded horn means the front wave is projected by the horn and the rear wave is projected by a port. **Fig. 4-22** Rear loading is just the opposite. The rear wave comes out the horn and the front wave is reflected. **Fig. 4-23** These are usually done with low frequency drivers.

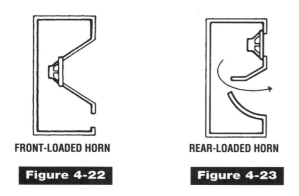

FRONT-LOADED HORN   REAR-LOADED HORN

Figure 4-22   **Figure 4-23**

As the length of a horn increases, the lower the frequency response. A horn with a 12" speaker can be tuned to 50 Hz. In order to achieve that cut-off frequency, the length of the horn would have to be eight feet and the area at the mouth of the horn would have to be over 40 square feet. Obviously, a horn this size would be impractical.

Folded horns are long horns designed to achieve certain bass frequency characteristics and are then reduced in size by a series of folds. This forces the wave to travel the length of the long horn, but in a compact area. Folded horns can be front or rear loaded also. **Fig. 4-24**

FOLDED HORN

Figure 4-24

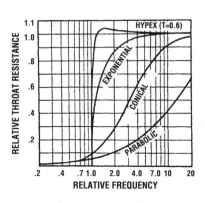

THROAT

MOUTH

FLARE

Figure 4-25

Horns are also used for mid range and high frequencies. Horns have three factors which effect their operation: a throat, a flare, and a mouth. **Fig. 4-25** The throat is the area where the driver connects. The flare is the rate at which the horn expands, and the mouth is the outer end. Different flare rates determine frequency cutoff points. The throat determines how much load is placed on the driver.

Different flare rates will produce different frequency response characteristics. The most common types of flare rates are hyperbolic, exponential, and conical. Each horn has its own performance capabilities. The hyperbolic curve has the slowest expansion, yet has the greatest low frequency response. The conical, on the other hand, expands quickly but has the poorest low end performance. An exponential has characteristics between the two. **Fig. 4-26**

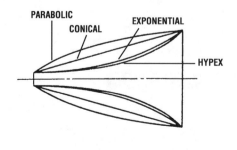

Figure 4-26

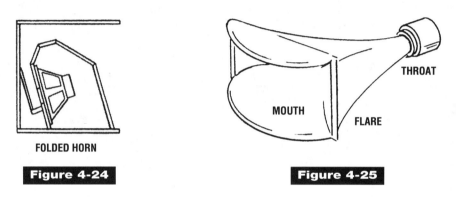

Although it may seem that the hyperbolic horn would have the greatest benefit, there is another problem to be discussed. Because of the slow expansion, there is high pressure at the throat area of the horn. This causes non-linear distortion again if sudden high energy bursts of low frequencies are fed to the horn.

Probably the best compromise is the exponential horn. It has a smooth frequency response and yet it minimizes this non-linear distortion.

Constant directivity horns are a relatively new type of horn. Typically, as frequencies increase, the direction of the horn narrows like water coming out of a garden hose. This tendency is known as beaming or high directivity. Constant directivity means that regardless of the frequency being reproduced, the dispersion pattern remains the same. **Fig. 4-27**

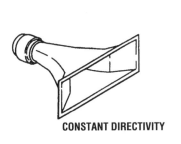

CONSTANT DIRECTIVITY

MULTICELLULAR

ACOUSTIC LENS

Figure 4-27

Speaker Cabinet Factors

There are many factors to consider when designing a P.A. system. A little knowledge and confidence can make a great deal of difference in how the system sounds. It can also save you a lot of money and headaches.

EFFICIENCY AND SENSITIVITY

Like drivers, speaker systems have different levels of efficiency. There are two basic ways to increase overall system SPL. One is to buy a lot of power amps, the other is to use efficient speakers. Efficiency refers to how much sound is actually produced and how much energy was dissipated into heat. Efficiency is usually rated as a percentage. For example, a good direct radiating speaker should have an efficiency rating of above 5%, while a good compression driver/horn combination should be above 25% efficiency. The most efficient speaker systems let the speakers do the work - not the power amps.

Most manufacturers publish a specification called sensitivity or SPL. This is a test performed by sending a full range signal (swept sine wave or pink noise) through the speaker at one watt of power. A sound pressure level meter is held one meter away (3.3 feet) and a reading is obtained.

A speaker with a rating of 106 dB will be louder than a speaker of 103 dB. In fact, it would require twice the power through the second speaker to be as loud as the first. (Remember the 3 dB = double the power rule)

POWER HANDLING CAPACITY

Power handling refers to how much power the speaker can handle without damage. This will be important to determine how much power is needed, not how loud the speaker will become. Power handling can be determined by a number of different ratings. The two most common ratings are Program and Continuous.

Continuous power (often called RMS) refers to a pure sine wave driving the speaker. Program power is a signal that is constantly changing, like program music. The program power rating is usually twice the continuous power because program music will reach peaks which the speaker can handle for short periods of time. Continuous sine waves make the speaker work continuously and therefore will burn it out faster. In either case, this information is critical when determining a system's power amplification needs and capacity.

FREQUENCY RESPONSE

Frequency response refers to the way a speaker reproduces frequencies across the entire audio spectrum. Speakers that have a "colored" sound should not necessarily be used for sound reinforcement. The ideal frequency response would be a flat line across the entire audio spectrum. Since this is unrealistic, you should look for a smooth curve avoiding "hot spots" which will modify the sound.

Many speaker manufacturers publish seemingly perfect frequency response ratings, from 20–20,000 Hz. While the speaker may reproduce notes throughout this range, how equally they are reproduced is another factor. Usually there is +/– variance given in dB which tells how "flat" the speaker really is. The less dB change throughout the range, the less variance of different frequencies. A speaker having a frequency response of 50–16,000 Hz +/–3 dB is much more effective than one with 20–20,000 Hz +/–10 dB. **Fig. 5-1**

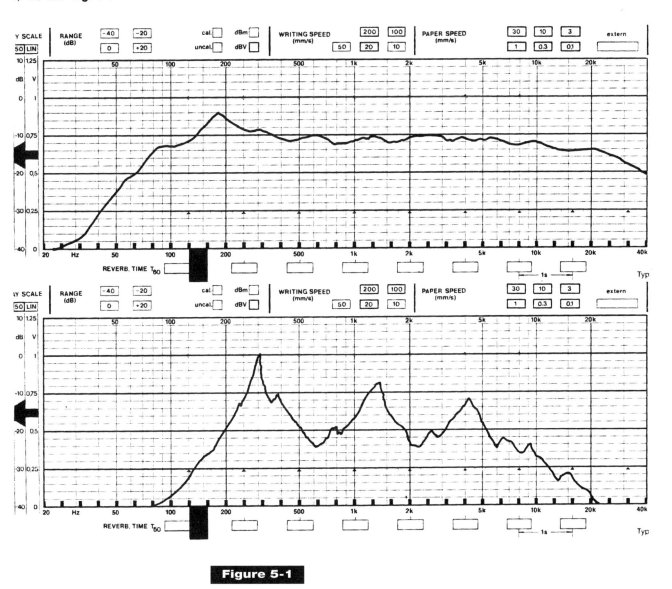

Figure 5-1

If the application is primarily for vocal use, the bass frequency response needs to go down to about 100 Hz. However, if music is being reproduced, the response should extend down to 40–50 Hz.

DISPERSION AND DIRECTIVITY

Low frequencies are virtually omni-directional. That is, they spread out in all directions because of the size of their wavelength. A 50 Hz tone, for instance, has a wavelength of 22.6 feet. That is considerably larger than the 15" cone driver so the sound spreads out in all directions.

As frequencies increase and wavelengths become smaller than the driver, sound tends to have a very narrow dispersion. The effect is called beaming and explains why the sound in front of the speaker is much clearer than off to the side. **Fig. 5-2**

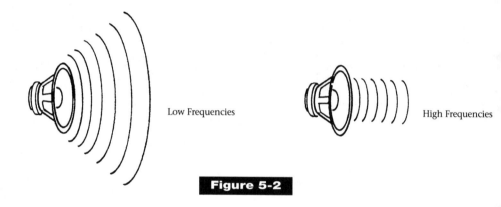

Low Frequencies   High Frequencies

Figure 5-2

Many manufacturers publish a specification called dispersion or coverage. This is usually given with horizontal and vertical degree measurements. For example, a cabinet with a rated coverage of 90° x 40°, means it will spread out sound 90 degrees horizontally and 40 degrees vertically. As you go outside this area, frequency response falls off.

It is important to realize that this measurement is an average measurement and it refers to a certain range of frequencies. It is better to get dispersion patterns of all the components in the enclosure and the frequency ranges covered by those components.

Directivity refers to the frequency response throughout a certain dispersion pattern. Constant directivity horns are relatively new but powerful devices. They can have wide or narrow dispersion patterns but they maintain a consistent frequency response throughout that pattern. That is, the sound off axis is as clear as on axis. While there may be a drop in signal level, the directivity of the horn remains constant. **Fig. 5-3**

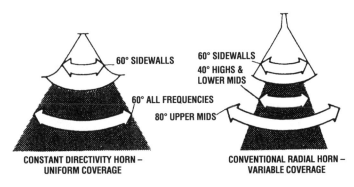

FIGURE 5-3 – Horizontal (Side-to-Side) Coverage Angle Comparison, Constant Directivity and Conventional Radial Horns

Figure 5-3

DISTANCE AND REVERBERATION

Two common problems facing audio engineers in system design are room reverbera-tion and distance. All rooms have, to some extent, a phenomenon called reverbera-tion. This characteristic is the tendency for sound to continue after the original sound has ceased. It is caused by sound waves bouncing around the room and hitting the ear at slightly different intervals.

The "reverberant field" is where the reverberated sound is actually louder than the original sound source. This makes the sound unintelligible and difficult to under-stand. Unfortunately, SPL in the reverberant field tends to remain constant no matter where you're standing in it. **Fig. 5-4**

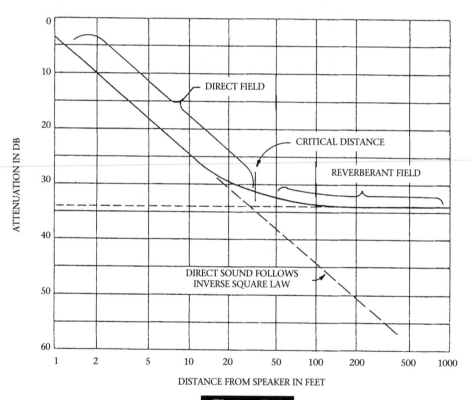

Figure 5-4

Parallel Connections

Parallel connections mean hooking up speakers to an amplifier the same way every time (all the positives to the positive and all the negatives to the negative). **Fig. 6-2** The load placed on the amplifier is increased with each additional speaker. As the load is increased, (impedance lowered), the amplifier puts out more power. If the load is increased too much, the amplifier will create too much power for itself and will over-heat. The amplifier manufacturer supplies a recommended minimal load impedance.

The formula for determining total load impedance is:

$$1 / (1/R_1 + 1/R_2 + \ldots + 1/R_n)$$

where "R" is the speaker impedance.

Parallel: 2/8 Ohm Speakers = 4 Ohm Load

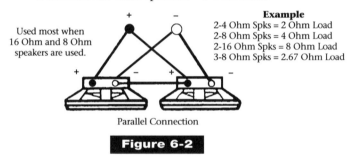

Used most when 16 Ohm and 8 Ohm speakers are used.

Example
2-4 Ohm Spks = 2 Ohm Load
2-8 Ohm Spks = 4 Ohm Load
2-16 Ohm Spks = 8 Ohm Load
3-8 Ohm Spks = 2.67 Ohm Load

Parallel Connection

Figure 6-2

So using two 8 ohm speakers in combination with one 16 ohm speaker would be:

$1 / (1/8 + 1/8 + 1/16) = 1 / (.125 + .125 + .0625) = 1 / .3125 = 3.2$ total load impedance.

Series/Parallel Connections

Sometimes it may be desirable to use a larger number of speakers without changing the total load impedance. Series/parallel connections allow sub-grouping of speakers in order to achieve any needed load impedance. To figure the total impedance, group all the series connections together and add the impedances of each speaker within each series group. Next, treat each series group as a single value and connect all series group in parallel using the parallel charts. **Fig. 6-3A**

For example, using four 8-ohm speakers, two groups of two speakers can be combined in series creating two 16-ohm subgroups. Hooking these in parallel would produce a total load impedance of 8-ohms.

Series/Parallel: 4/8 Ohm Speakers = 8 Ohm Load

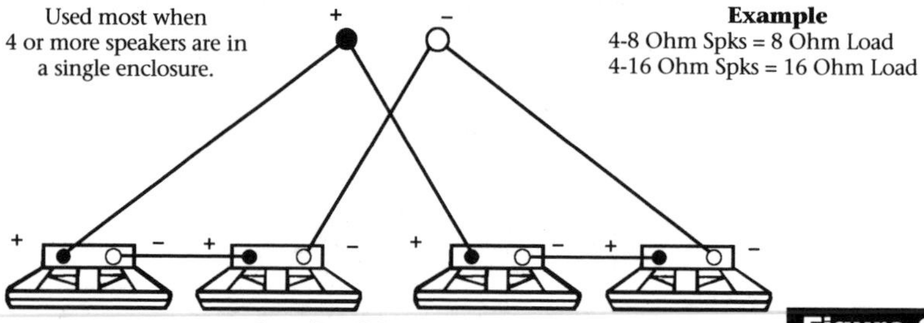

Used most when
4 or more speakers are in
a single enclosure.

Example
4-8 Ohm Spks = 8 Ohm Load
4-16 Ohm Spks = 16 Ohm Load

Series/Parallel Connection

Figure 6-3A

Here is a table to calculate the total load impedance of common speaker combinations.

Fig. 6-3B

IMPEDANCE COMBINING TABLE

			SYSTEM ONE								
			SINGLE SPEAKER			TWO SPEAKERS IN PARALLEL					
			4	8	16	4:4	4:8	4:16	8:8	8:16	16:16
S Y S T E M T W O	SINGLE SPKR	4	2	2.7	3.2	*1.3*	*1.6*	*1.8*	2	2.3	2.7
		8	2.7	4	5.3	*1.6*	2	2.3	2.7	3.2	4
		16	3.2	5.3	8	*1.8*	2.3	2.7	3.2	4	5.3
	TWO SPKRS IN PARALLEL	4:4	*1.3*	*1.6*	*1.8*	*1*	*1.1*	*1.2*	*1.3*	*1.5*	*1.6*
		4:8	*1.6*	2	2.3	*1.1*	*1.3*	*1.5*	*1.6*	*1.8*	2
		4:16	*1.8*	2.3	2.7	*1.2*	*1.5*	*1.6*	*1.8*	2	2.3
		8:8	2	2.7	3.2	*1.3*	*1.6*	*1.8*	2	2.3	2.7
		8:16	2.3	3.2	4	*1.5*	*1.8*	2	2.3	2.7	3.2
		16:16	2.7	4	5.3	*1.6*	2	2.3	2.7	3.2	4

Figure 6-3B

ASTERISKS (*) INDICATE COMBINATIONS RESULTING
IN IMPEDANCES LESS THAN TWO OHMS.
THESE COMBINATIONS ARE NOT RECOMMENDED AND MAY LEAD TO REDUCED
POWER OUTPUT OR EXCESS DISTORTION

POWER OUTPUT

The power output of an amplifier changes as the total load impedance increases or decreases. That is why on manufacturer's specifications it is important to know the rated power into how many ohms. An amplifier claiming to produce 500 watts may be able to do that only when you hook up 8 speakers in parallel.

Most speaker cabinets are designed with an 8 ohm input impedance. Let's say an amplifier has a rated power output of 200 watts into 4 ohms and a minimal load impedance of 2 ohms. If one 8-ohm input speaker is used, the amplifier will produce only about 100 watts. Using two 8-ohm speakers in parallel will place a 4-ohm total load impedance and the amplifier will produce 200 watts, approximately doubling the power by adding one speaker!

If a 2-ohm total load impedance was used (four 8-ohm cabinets), the amplifier would try to double the power again. Because of factors such as additional internal resistance caused by the increase in current, the actual power produced would be around 360 watts.

If four more 8-ohm cabinets were added, the total impedance would drop down to 1-ohm. This is below the recommended minimal load impedance and would cause the amplifier to overheat, distort, or burn up. Some amplifiers have built in protection which shuts the unit down when impedance is lowered beyond safe operating limits. This is because the amplifier would try to double the power, but the components in the amplifier were not designed for that level of power.

POWER OUTPUT PER SPEAKER

Every time a speaker is added in parallel, the amplifier develops more power. Two speakers with the same input impedance will divide the total power equally between the cabinets. For example, using the amplifier mentioned above, if four 8-ohm speakers were connected, the total output power is 360 watts. Each 8-ohm speaker would accept 90 watts (360/4). If two 8-ohm speakers were used, the two would split the 200 watts produced (100 watts apiece).

What happens with speakers having unlike impedances? Speakers with differently rated impedances will draw different amounts of power from the amplifier. Lower impedances mean less resistance and, therefore, more power to that speaker. To figure out the power output per speaker, divide the total load impedance by the individual speaker's rated impedance. Multiply that number by the total power output. Using our example power amp, a two ohm total load impedance was achieved by combining speakers with input impedances of 4, 8, 16, and 16 ohms. Since the total output power at two ohms is 360 watts, the individual speaker output power breaks down as follows:

Power delivered to speaker "n" = R_{total} / R_n x P_{total}

2/4 = 1/2 x 360 = 180 watts for the 4-ohm speaker

2/8 = 1/4 x 360 = 90 watts for the 8-ohm speaker

2/16 = 1/8 x 360 = 45 watts for the 16-ohm speaker

2/16 = 1/8 x 360 = 45 watts for the 16-ohm speaker

Notice that half of the total power output goes to the 4-ohm speaker because it has the least resistance; it impedes current flow the least. **Fig. 6-4**

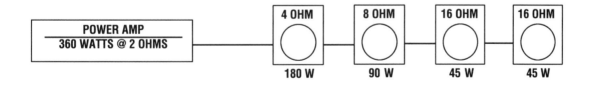

Figure 6-4

Power Amplifiers

Power amps have one particular function in sound reinforcement – to drive speakers. They are equivalent in P.A.'s as the engine is in our cars. They do work and supply power. Power amps can be built into a complete musical instrument amplifier or into a mixer, or as a free standing unit. Here is a typical specification sheet on a power amplifier. We will go through each feature and talk about what each specification really means.

RMA-1000 DETAILED SPECIFICATIONS

POWER OUTPUT:	150 Watts RMS @ 4 ohms, each channel, stereo 220 Watts RMS @ 2 ohms, each channel, stereo 300 Watts RMS @ 8 ohms, mono bridge 440 Watts RMS @ 4 ohms, mono bridge
FREQUENCY REPSONSE:	+0, –.25DB/20 hz–20K hz @ full rated power
TOTAL HARMONIC DISTORTION:	Less than .2%, 20 hz–20K hz @ 150W/4 ohm Typical .02% @ 1K hz
INTERMODULATION DISTORTION:	Less than .05% @ 150W/4 ohm
SLEW RATE:	25 Volts per micro-second
SIGNAL TO NOISE RATIO:	Greater than –100 DB from 150 watts
INPUT TYPE AND IMPEDANCE:	Transformerless electronically balanced, 20K actual load impedance. Suitable for Low or Hi-Z balanced line. 3 pin "XLR" + 1/4" phone jack input per channel.
INPUT SENSITIVITY:	1.0 V RMS for 150 watts, 4 ohms, (+2 DBM)
LOAD IMPEDANCE:	Will drive loads equal to 2 ohms or greater, stereo mode; 4 ohms or greater, mono bridge mode. Stable into any load configuration.
DAMPING FACTOR:	Typical 250 (1K hz, 8 ohms)
OUTPUT CONNECTIONS:	1/4" phone jack, +5 way binding posts each channel
PROTECTION CIRCUITRY:	Short circuit, RF burnout, overtemp, speaker protection relays – turn on/turn off transient protection, DC protection. Built-in auto limiter (anti-clip).
COOLING:	Forced air fan cooling, rear intake – front exhaust
POWER REQUIREMENTS:	120 VAC., 60 hz, 9 amps maximum

POWER OUTPUT

The two most popular types of power amps are monaural and stereo amplifiers. A monaural (mono) amp has one individual power amp while a stereo power amp is generally two individual power amps in one package. These two amps can be used independently or they can be used together to create more power. The latter feature is called bridging. (Many stereo amps can be used in a mono mode but they cannot necessarily be bridged to develop more power. Make certain that the amplifier has the ability to be bridged into a mono mode.)

Power can be rated by many different methods. All of them are based on the size or level of the amplified waveform. An amplifier is a multiplier and a small input signal from a mixer which has a level of one volt, might be amplified to 20 or 30 volts. An example of the amplified waveform is shown. **Fig. 7-1**

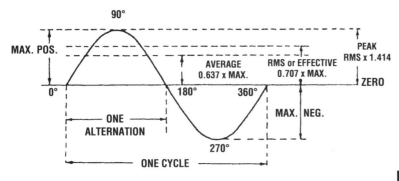

Figure 7-1

SINE-WAVE TERMINOLOGY AND VOLTAGE RELATIONS

This waveform has a peak of 20 volts and therefore a peak to peak rating of 40 volts. Other types of ratings include average which is .637 times the peak and root mean square (RMS) which is .707 times the peak. All of these ratings are mathematically related. Here is a chart of these relationships for a sine wave:

RMS = .707 x Peak
RMS = 1.11 x Avg.
Peak = 1.414 x RMS
Peak = 1.57 x Avg.
Avg. = .637 x Peak
Avg. = .9 x RMS
Peak to Peak = 2.828 x RMS
RMS = .3535 x Peak to Peak

RMS is the best method of rating the effective voltage, so it should be used for determining the power. Remember that power is simply the output voltage squared, and then divided by the resistance of the speaker(s). $P = E^2/R$

Using different voltage ratings such as peak to peak or peak will create more impressive specifications but it should be noted these ratings last only a few milliseconds and do not mean more audible sound. When comparing pieces of audio equipment use only the RMS rating.

Because power actually changes with impedance, it is important to know the levels of power at a given load impedance. For example, just because a power amp is rated at 800 watts, it doesn't mean you will get 800 watts. That rating will only be achieved if the proper load is placed on the amplifier. Power amps usually give a nominal (usual) recommended impedance and a minimal load impedance.

In our example spec sheet, it says the power output is 150 watts RMS @ 4 ohms and 220 watts @ 2 ohms for each channel. 4 ohms is the nominal impedance and 2 ohms is the minimal. If less than a two ohm load is used, the power amp would try to put out more power and would possibly overheat. Some power amps are severely damaged if they are operated under their recommended minimal impedance.

When the example amplifier is used in a bridged mode, it creates more power into higher impedances. That is because both channels of the amplifier are being used together to amplify a signal. Notice that the bridged rating is the sum of the two individual channel ratings. 150 watts @ 4 ohms + 150 watts @ 4 ohms = 300 watts @ 8 ohms. The minimal load impedance in the bridged mode is 4 ohms (two ohms per channel).

FREQUENCY RESPONSE

Because a power amp is suppose to reproduce input signals very accurately, there should be no tonal coloration of the sound. Frequency response of an amplifier should be as flat as possible throughout the entire audio spectrum (20–20k Hz). There should be a +/– variance published to show how smooth the response curve is. Many amplifier companies publish responses that range from 5 Hz to 50,000 Hz. While this may appear impressive, it's important to realize that the area you are most concerned with is the range which is audible to the ear and what the speaker can reproduce.

The frequency response measurement is made by sweeping a waveform throughout the entire spectrum and plotting it on a graph. It is important to note at what level the measurement was taken. In our example, the measurement was taken at full power, the most strenuous for the amp and was still flat within 1/4 of a decibel. Many amplifier companies often flatter themselves by taking this measurement at low power levels. This type of measurement may indicate that the amp is not flat at full power. In fact, it may have some severe dips in the frequency response. **Fig. 7-2**

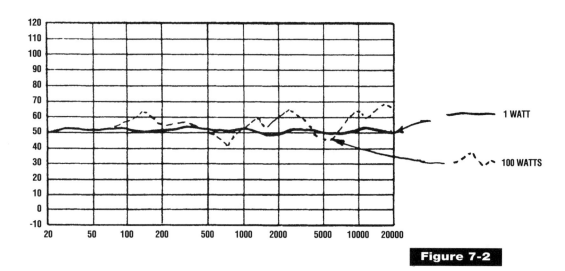

Figure 7-2

TOTAL HARMONIC DISTORTION (THD)

When an amp is at full power, there is typically a slight alteration of the output signal comparative to the input signal. This is caused by the amplifier producing a certain percentage of harmonics along with the original signal. These harmonics are "ghost tones" that are inherently generated by the amplifier. All the harmonic frequencies are related by whole number integers and therefore are musically related. Studies have shown that the human ear can withstand about 1% total harmonic distortion before it becomes annoying. (This percentage changes depending upon the source or program.) Everything else being equal, the lower the THD in the amp, the better.

INTERMODULATION DISTORTION (IMD)

Intermodulation distortion differs from harmonic distortion in that the resulting "ghost tones" are not musically related. Instead of being related by whole number multiples, the notes produced are sums and differences of two frequencies. Generally, 60 Hz and 7000 Hz test frequencies are played simultaneously. IMD would be ghost tones such as 6940 Hz and 7060 Hz and then sums and differences between all these new ghost tones. Intermodulation distortion is typically more annoying than harmonic distortion. Once again, everything else being equal, the lower the number, the better the specification.

SLEW RATE

Slew rate refers to how fast the amplifier responds to the input signal. It is measured in volts per microsecond and is similar to acceleration tests on cars. Suppose two cars were tested to see how fast they can accelerate in 10 seconds. Car A might go from 0 to 50 MPH and car B from 0 to 120 in the same 10 seconds. Obviously car B would have the greater performance specification.

While some audiophiles might argue that there is no upper limit or overkill, there is a formula which determines the minimum accepted slew rate for appropriate performance. That formula is:

$$2 \times \pi \times F \times PVO \ / \ 1,000,000$$

Where: $\pi = 3.1416$

F = test frequency

PVO = peak voltage output of the amplifier

As frequency increases, the required slew rate also increases. So an amplifier with a peak voltage output of 25 volts being tested at 20,000 Hz should have a slew rate of 3.14 volts per microsecond. (2 x 3.1416 x 20,000 x 25 / 1,000,000 = 3.14) The amplifier in our example which has a peak voltage output of about 25 volts has a more than adequate slew rate of 25 volts per microsecond.

SIGNAL TO NOISE RATIO

Every piece of electronic equipment has inherent noise called thermal or Gaussian noise. While there is no way to get rid of this noise, it is possible to have the music signal so much greater in level that the noise would be unnoticeable. The standard minimum acceptable signal to noise ratio in sound reinforcement equipment is 65 dB. In our example, the amplifier has a signal to noise ratio of over 100 dB.

INPUT SENSITIVITY

Input sensitivity refers to the minimum input signal strength required for the amplifier to produce full RMS power. If the output of a mixer is .775 volts and the input sensitivity of a power amp is one volt, there is no way for the amp to reach full power. Because of that fact, many power amps have input level controls built in. These controls are often confused with volume controls. They do affect the loudness of the amplifier but only by adjusting the level of the incoming signal. In the above example with the mixer output of .775, we might be able to increase the gain of the power amp to accept the one volt level by using the gain control on the amp.

DAMPING FACTOR

Damping factor (the rated load impedance divided by the sum of the internal output impedance of the amplifier and the DC resistance of the voice coil) refers to the ability of the amplifier to control precisely the speaker's movement. Generally the higher the number, the greater the control the amp has over the speaker, and therefore, the more accurate the response. In general, any rating over twenty (20) is considered acceptable. The amplifier in our example has a damping factor of 250.

PROTECTION CIRCUITRY

Many amplifiers have built in circuitry to protect the unit from various problems. Common protection circuitry include the following:

1. **Short Circuit Protection.** If the speaker wire shorts out or the speaker terminals are accidentally hooked together, a short circuit exists. This poses no resistance to the amplifier's output and damage could occur. Short circuit protection prevents damage to the amp if the speaker output terminals are shorted.

2. **RF Burnout.** Radio frequencies are constantly bouncing around in the air. Some circuitry in the amplifier may act like a receiver and pick up certain radio frequencies. As the amp tries to reproduce this ultra-high frequency signal, it may overheat and become damaged. RF burnout protection refers to a protective circuit which prevents the amplifier from trying to reproduce radio frequencies.

3. **Overtemp Protection.** As any power amp works, it creates heat as a by-product. Too much heat can cause the amp to fail. Many amplifiers use heat sinks, large metal surfaces which are in contact with the air. The air then cools off these metal heat sinks.

   Another type of heat protection is mounting a fan in the amplifier itself. The fan draws in cool air and blows out hot air. Many amplifiers have dual speed fans which regulate air circulation as required by the amp.

   Some amplifiers have a thermal relay in the amplifier which turns off the amplifier if excessive temperatures are reached. On amplifiers with fans, this thermal relay should turn off the speakers but allow the fan to continue to operate.

4. **Turn off/on Transient Protection.** When an amplifier is turned on, the electronic components come on line. It may take a second or two for all voltage levels to stabilize. This unstable state can cause a "thump" to be amplified and sent to the speakers which could damage high frequency components. Transient protection uses a relay which waits a few seconds before the speaker terminals are connected. This prevents any "thumps" or "pops" from getting to the speaker.

5. **DC Detector.** DC (direct current) is bad for a speaker. It says to the speaker "move in one direction only". This creates strain on the speaker and can quickly destroy it. Many amplifiers have electronic circuitry which senses DC and disconnects the speaker terminals to protect the speakers.

6. **Fuses.** Fuses can be used to protect two areas of the amp. The first fuse protects the amp from excessive current coming in via the main AC line. The second fuse(s) protects individual circuits like the pre-amp and power amp from excessive current from the amplifier's power supply.

   If a fuse ever blows, be sure to replace it with the same value fuse. If the amplifier continues to blow fuses, take it to a qualified service center.

7. **Limiters.** One of the most important features in an amplifier is a device called a limiter. An amplifier is a multiplier and if a large input signal is presented to the amp, it will be multiplied by the same multiplication factor. But amplifiers have a limit to which they will amplify preset by voltage limits. If a signal is larger than these voltage limits, distortion will occur. A limiter is a device which puts a ceiling on how much the signal will be amplified. This level is within the voltage limits and thereby prevents any clipping of the waveform. **Fig. 7-3**

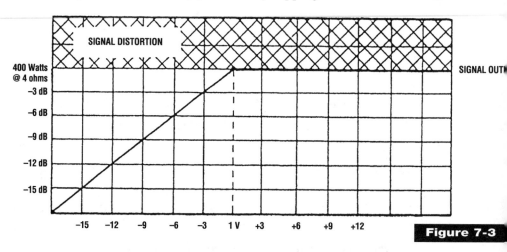

Figure 7-3

MATCHING POWER AMPS WITH SPEAKERS

A common cause for "blown" speaker components is too much power being sent to that component. The solution to this might seem to be using a power amp with a power output less than the total handling capacity of all the cabinets. This may cause even more blown components. How is that possible?

Most tweeters require less power than woofers because they are more efficient than cone loudspeakers. Because tweeters must be lightweight, they cannot handle large amounts of power compared to larger cone drivers. Suppose we have a two-way cabinet with a 100 watt handling capacity. The woofer will be able to handle 100 watts by itself, but the tweeter may be rated at only 10 watts.

This power separation between woofer and tweeter is accomplished by a passive crossover in the cabinet which has a power handling capacity of 100 watts. This crossover sends lows to the woofer and highs to the tweeter in the proper power percentages. No problem so far. This system will work fine as long as the signal sent to the cabinet is clean (no distortion). **Fig. 7-4**

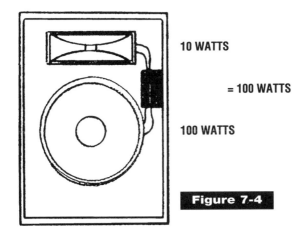

10 WATTS

= 100 WATTS

100 WATTS

Figure 7-4

If a 100 watt amplifier is used with two of the above speakers, each speaker will receive 50 watts. The problem is when that amplifier is driven to full output, distortion will probably occur (unless the amp is exceptionally clean or has protective circuitry like a limiter to prevent distortion). When distortion develops, a major increase in harmonics occurs causing an unbalance of high frequencies to be sent to the tweeters. In fact, the tweeters can receive as much as twice the amount of normal power distribution. Over an extended period of time, the excessive harmonics produced will blow the tweeters.

So, rather than driving a small power amp to full RMS output, use a larger power amp that will develop full output on peaks only. It is a common rule to use an amp capable of producing twice the power that you will need. This extra power is the concept of headroom. Headroom is the reserve power needed for peaks. Remember speaker power handling capacity ratings, they are given in continuous and program. The difference between the two is headroom in the speaker.

HEADROOM

Because a power amp is rated at a certain wattage does not mean that amp will be continually putting out that power. In fact, a high quality music sound system should have 10–40dB of headroom. So if a 200 watt amplifier is used, most of the time it will be putting out between only 2–20 watts! (10 dB is equal to 10 times the power) The remaining power is required for peaks in the program. If a 200 watt amp is being used and you're constantly "clipping" or over-driving it, you need to get a larger amp or an amp with a limiter. Otherwise, you will have distortion sent to your speakers which can damage them.

Sound Reinforcement System Interconnection

The popular P.A. (public address) system of the 1960's was a "box" head, usually with only four channels, and a pair of column speakers. This system, epitomized by the Shure VocalMaster, was used to amplify the vocalists and was used by the best bands in town. As the power level of equipment grew, there was a need to establish balance among the musicians. It was also desirable to "mix" the inputs in order to have control of the overall output.

The quality and affordability of today's sound systems have progressed so much that even garage bands are now enjoying a high fidelity sound that would have been associated only with the finest recording studios. Part of the reason is ease of operation on many pieces of modern equipment. Unfortunately, there are many connections and adjustments that require some decision making on the owner's part. However, knowing a few basic rules can provide any "sound man" with enough ammunition to achieve quality sound reproduction.

Today's sound systems are made up of many components. As in the stereo industry, the sound technician will typically piece together a system to fit the needs of the band, rather than buy an "all-in-one" package. These components include not only the mixer, power amps, and speakers, but the microphones and amplified instruments. Even the musician should be considered a variable in the system because playing styles can also affect the output of the system.

PATCHING EQUIPMENT

Terms used in patching together components include source, input, output, and load. An example of a complete chain would be a microphone as a source to the input of a powered mixer. From the output of the powered mixer to the load or speaker.

Note that these connections are relative to one another. The input of the powered mixer can be thought of as the load for the microphone, while the output of the powered mixer can also be viewed as the source for the speaker's input. Therefore, the mixer has input and output impedance ratings. Input impedance is also known as load impedance and output impedance is commonly referred to as source impedance. These terms and relative nature are important in understanding impedance and level matching.

The first and most obvious rule of making connections is to match inputs with outputs. It is important, however, to make sure these inputs and outputs are compatible. This is known as impedance and level matching.

IMPEDANCE MATCHING

Impedance, as we have learned, simply means the property of resisting or controlling the current flow. Impedance matching, in its original meaning, refers to having identical impedances at the output and input of connecting devices; matching source and load impedances. This stems back from the days when telephones were voice power operated - the louder you talked, the better the signal sent. The sound was also better when the telephone line impedance (600 ohms) was equal to the transmitter impedance. This started the concept of exactly matching impedances.

This belief was further complicated by tube amplifiers having to be identically matched to the speaker's load impedance. If the two were not matched, the output tube or the transformer would burn up. Many tube amplifiers are still just as picky.

With most modern solid state equipment, exact matching is unnecessary. There are a few rules of thumb that should be followed. To illustrate these rules, let's walk through a sequence in the audio chain.

1. **Microphone to mixer -** All microphones have a published source impedance which is the inherent resistance within the circuit itself. Microphones are usually categorized as low impedance (under 600 ohms) or high impedance (over 600 but as high as 100,000 ohms). Mixer inputs will have a rated input or load impedance. How can a mixer accept these different types of microphones with such a wide variance in source impedance? Luckily, impedance matching in most cases can be renamed impedance watching. That is, the source impedance for a microphone does not have to match exactly the input impedance of the mixer. A rule of thumb is that the input impedance of the mixer should be five to ten times greater than the source impedance of the microphone.

   So a microphone having a source impedance of 250 ohms (a common rating) will work properly in a mixer's input having a load impedance of 1250 ohms or greater up to about 2500 ohms.

2. **Mixer to power amp -** An unpowered mixer must be connected to a power amplifier. As with the microphone, the mixer will have a published output (source) impedance. Likewise, the power amp will have a rated input impedance. The rule of thumb for connecting any type of "active devices" is making sure the input impedance exceeds the output impedance. An active device is defined as any unit requiring a battery or AC power.

   For example, a mixer with an output impedance of 600 ohms needs to operate into an amplifier with an input impedance of at least that. If this rule is not followed, excessive distortion could occur. Most power amps or other line level devices such as delays, limiters, or graphic equalizers will have input impedances well above the output of any mixer. A line level device is one whose signal output is from around .5V to 10V.

3. **Power amp to speakers -** Most power amps rate not only their speaker output impedance, but also list their minimum acceptable load impedance. The general rule here is to never operate under the minimal load impedance rated on the amp, because distortion, and in some cases, equipment failure, will occur.

   Speakers usually have rated input impedances of 4, 8, or 16 ohms. Using multiple speakers will change the total load impedance which the amplifier "sees". But with a power amp having a nominal load impedance rating of 8 ohms and a minimal load impedance of 4 ohms, many combination of speakers can be used as long as the total load impedance is not less than 4 ohms. (See Chapter Six.)

Impedances and Cables

Cable and wire by themselves add resistance, and can also affect the signal. In particular, cable in lengths of roughly 15 feet or more do a better job of transmitting some frequency ranges than others. This is due to an electrical property called capacitance. Long wire carrying high impedance signals tend to lose or "roll off" high frequencies, making voice reproduction dull and unintelligible. Long wire carrying low impedance signals also roll off high frequencies, but only those which are well above the audible range. Therefore, whenever long cables are required, low impedance sources should be used.

Speaker cable (unshielded) also adds resistance and if long speaker cables are used, some of the power will actually be lost in the cable. Using larger wire and shorter speaker cable length will dramatically improve power amp/speaker performance. In order to accomplish this:

1. Keep power amps close to speakers.

2. Use heavy gauge speaker cables. The smaller the number, the thicker the wire; #14 is bigger than #20.

3. Use unshielded cable for speaker connections.

The charts on this page will assist you in selection of proper wire conductor sizes and lengths for use with power amplifiers into various load impedances. Improper wiring can and will cause loss of power and/or efficiency in speaker hookup to power amplifiers. Chart one shows the total resistance of various lengths of cable in the different wire gauges. Chart two shows the lengths of cable in the various wire gauges that will cause one and three dB drops in power delivered to the speaker. Chart three shows the maximum recommended lengths of the various wire gauges at different impedance loads in order to assure minimal effect on "SPL" or power output to speakers.

Chart One - Wire length versus resistance of cable								
Awg	Ohms*	1000	500	250	125	100	50	25
#14	.0052	5.20	2.60	1.30	.65	.52	.26	.13
#18	.0131	13.10	6.55	3.28	1.64	1.31	.66	.33
#20	.0207	20.70	10.35	5.18	2.59	2.07	1.04	.52
#24	.0524	52.40	26.20	13.10	6.55	5.24	2.62	1.31

*Ohms per foot based on total of wire pair.

Chart Two - Cable length for 1 and 3 dB line losses					
	2 Ω load		4 Ω load		8 Ω load	
Awg #	– 3 dB	–1 dB	–3 dB	–1 dB	–3 dB	–1 dB
#14	159	47	319	94	637	188
#18	63	19	126	37	253	75
#20	40	12	80	24	160	47
#24	16	5	32	9	63	19

Chart Three - Maximum recommended cable lengths			
Awg #	2 Ω	4 Ω	8 Ω
#14	25	50	100
#18	15	30	60
#20	10	20	40
#24	6	12	24

General Rules

We have seen that for most modern equipment, impedance matching at most connections does not have to be exact. But it is important that the input and output impedances are compatible from the power amp to the speakers. Following a few basic rules will ensure maximum development of power without damage to components, and will allow clean, quiet operation.

1. **Always connect "up" into the input impedance.**

2. **Never connect high impedance sources (outputs) to low impedance loads (inputs).**

3. **The only time you have to exactly match impedances is when specified by the equipment's manufacturer (as with some tube amplifiers).**

4. **Amplifiers develop more power as the load impedance of the speakers drop. However, never go below the manufacturers recommended minimal load impedance.**

SIGNAL MATCHING

In sound reinforcement applications, a critical link in the quality sound reproduction chain is component signal matching. Signal matching simply means having the output level of each source be neither too strong or too weak for optimum operation of each subsequent input.

Improper signal matching generates two potential problems—distortion and noise. **Fig. 8-1**

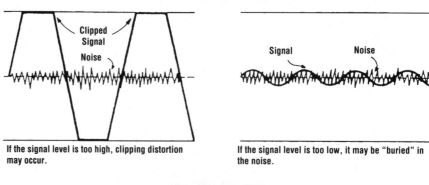

If the signal level is too high, clipping distortion may occur.

If the signal level is too low, it may be "buried" in the noise.

Figure 8-1

Distortion: When too much signal is supplied to an input, the limitations of that input are exceeded and distortion occurs. The more the limit is exceeded, the more distortion occurs. (Guitar players like this sound and that is why when the channel gain of an amplifier is turned to 10, overdrive or distortion is heard).

Every electronic circuit has inherent "hiss" to it. This is called thermal or Gaussian noise. It is not hum or buzzing, it is like the sound heard in between stations on the radio. There is no way to totally eliminate this noise. Instead, the signal should be maximized in order to obtain a high SIGNAL-TO-NOISE ratio. In other words, if the signal is much louder than the noise, the noise will not be heard. If an input signal is too weak, the signal-to-noise ratio is reduced and hiss occurs.

Signal Classifications

There are three classifications of signal levels in audio equipment:

Fig. 8-2

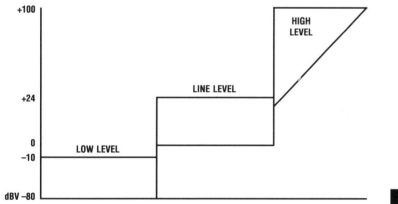

Figure 8-2

- **Low level devices** — those developing only millivolts like microphones or guitar pickups.

- **Line level devices** — those usually requiring some type of external power like graphic equalizers, delays, and tape decks. Line level devices operate at the level around one volt.

- **High level devices** — those developing voltage into resistance and creating power, like the speaker output of an amplifier.

Unless specified by manufacturer, NEVER connect devices from one classification to another. For example, you shouldn't plug a microphone directly into a power amp. The microphone's output is too low. This connection would result in very low, if any, output from the amplifier.

You also shouldn't plug the speaker out of a power amp into the input of a mixer. The large amount of voltage produced by the power amp could damage the input of the mixer.

Many devices accept an input of one classification and then boost the output to another classification. For example, a mixer's input accepts low level signals, while the same mixer's output is probably line level. A power amp input is line level while its output is high level.

On a specification sheet, the connection stages are listed input level, input voltage, input sensitivity, maximum signal accepted, etc. Outputs are listed the same way. These ratings are usually given in dB or volts.

Voltage Rated in Decibels

We have seen that decibels can be used to measure sound pressure levels. They can also be used to determine power ratios. Because of their comparative nature, they can be used in any measuring system. Unfortunately, the "3 dB = twice as much" rule used for power does not apply to voltage. Instead, a new ratio scale for voltage is used.

As with any decibel measurement, the dB scale must use a reference figure. There are two commonly used dB voltage references: dBV, where 0 dB is equal to one volt, and dBu (also called dBv) where 0 dB is equal to .775 volts. Don't panic! The two different dB voltage references are used for specific reasons and applications.

dBV

dBV is used for any voltage comparison. Voltage ratios are based on 6 dB = twice the voltage instead of our power ratio where 3 dB = twice the power.

Here is a chart which lists the relationships between power and both voltage ratios.

dB	POWER (watts)	VOLTAGE (volts)	VOLTAGE (volts into 600 ohms)
0	1	1	1.2
1	1.3	1.1	1.4
2	1.6	1.3	1.6
3	2	1.4	1.8
4	2.5	1.6	2
5	3.2	1.8	2.3
6	4	2	2.5
7	5	2.2	2.9
8	6.3	2.5	3.2
9	8	2.8	3.6
10	10	3.2	4
11	12.6	3.5	4.5
12	16	4	5.1
15	32	5.6	7.2
18	64	8	10.2
20	100	10	12.8
30	1000	31.6	40.7
40	10000	100	128.8
50	100000	316.2	407.3
60	1000000	1000	1288.2
70	10000000	3162.3	4073.8
80	100000000	10000	128825
90	1000000000	31622.8	407380
100	10000000000	100000	1288250
110	100000000000	316227.8	4073800
120	1000000000000	1000000	12882500
	dBW 10log (P/1 watt)	dBV 20log (V/1 volt)	dBu or dBv 20log (V/.775 volt)

dBu

Since dB can be used to compare voltage, a common scale in matching equipment is called dBu where zero dBu (sometimes called dBv) is referenced to .775 volts. This number is not an arbitrary reference, but is a common number found in sound reinforcement equipment. When a mixer produces one milliwatt of power (1/1000 watt) into 600 ohms, the voltage level is .775 volts. But why 600 ohms and one milliwatt? That stems back once again to the phone company and the impedance of the old telephones. Thus, the .775 reference is common in sound reinforcement and recording equipment.

dBu	Volts	dBu	Volts
0	.775	−1	.690
+1	.870	−2	.615
+2	.976	−3	.548
+3	1.10	−4	.488
+4	1.23	−5	.435
+5	1.38	−6	.387
+6	1.55	−7	.346
+7	1.74	−8	.308
+8	1.95	−9	.277
+9	2.19	−10	.242
+10	2.46	−11	.221
+11	2.75	−12	.193
+12	3.09	−15	.138
+15	4.36	−18	.097
+18	6.16	−20	.077
+20	7.75		

Matching Signal Levels

The specification chart of a mixer may read:

Max. signal level accepted.............6 volts RMS (+18 dBv)

Input sensitivity.............................2 millivolts (–52 dBv)

The maximum signal accepted is the highest value the mixer can use without excessive distortion. The input sensitivity is the smallest amount of signal required for the mixer to operate. As you can see, this is quite a range (70 dB).

All mixers are designed to operate best at a nominal or normal level. This is the level where the signal-to-noise ratio is maximized while still preventing distortion. The difference between the nominal operating level and clipping is called headroom. Headroom can be considered reserve power, as in your car. The legal speed limit on U.S. highways is 55 miles per hour. Your car easily operates at that speed. However, if you have to pass someone, you need the ability to achieve more speed without damage to the engine.

Suppose we have a microphone and a tape deck which we wish to connect to the mixer. The nominal output of the microphone is two millivolts, while the nominal output of the tape deck is six volts. Both will operate in the mixer, but because their levels are at the maximum and minimal ranges of the mixer, some problems may occur. The mixer could be designed to operate nominally for either input, but again, we could have some problems.

If the mixer described here was designed to operate nominally at two millivolts for the microphone, using the tape recorder would overdrive or clip the input causing distortion. On the other hand, if the mixer was designed to accept the six volt input, using an input like the microphone would require so much boosting it would cause electronic noise or hiss.

How do we compensate for this wide range of inputs? Many mixers have a control in the pre-amp stage marked TRIM, GAIN, ATTENUATION, PAD, etc. This control allows the user to adjust the level of the incoming signal to achieve a workable signal-to-noise ratio while still preserving headroom.

Most line level device manufacturers have standardized input and output levels so signal matching is much easier. Common nominal input and output levels are –20 dB, –10 dB, and +4 dB. These devices usually have controls or designated input jacks to facilitate these different levels.

PADS, PREAMPS, AND TRANSFORMERS

In many instances, connection of existing equipment may cause excessive noise or distortion due to mismatched impedances or gain. If your equipment does not have a variable gain control, or if the impedance mismatch is unacceptable, accessories are available or can be constructed to solve these problems.

A pad is a circuit which reduces the output level of a source to make it compatible with the input of another device. They are necessary when a source's output is too strong for an input. For example, if a graphic equalizer's output was +4 dBv and the input of a power amp was –10 dBv, a –14 dB pad would be required to match the signal levels.

A pre-amp is just the opposite of a pad. It boosts a weak signal to the level required by an input. If the output of an acoustic guitar pickup was –50 dBv and the mixer's input had a nominal input of –20 dBv, a 30 dB pre-amp should be used to boost the pickup.

Transformers are used to convert impedances and levels. For example, a "high Z to low Z" microphone transformer converts the high impedance and high voltage level of a high impedance microphone to low impedance and low level. These are commonly used to allow use of long microphone cables with high impedance microphones.

BALANCED VS. UNBALANCED

A common misconception about microphones is that low impedance microphones are balanced and high impedance are unbalanced. That is not necessarily the case. In fact, impedance and balanced have nothing to do with each other except that most manufacturers of microphones tend to link the two features together. It is not uncommon to have an unbalanced, low impedance microphone. And it's also possible to have a balanced, high impedance microphone.

Balanced and Unbalanced Lines

Because audio signals travel as an alternating current, at least two wires are always required to complete the circuit. An unbalanced line has one audio signal carrying wire wrapped by another wire. This outer wire also acts as a shield against extraneous noises such as radio frequencies, static, hum, or hiss. The shield carries both noise and signal, noise on the outside of the wire, signal on the inside. The line is said to be unbalanced because the levels of signal on each wire is unequal. While this type of cable eliminates noise, some noise will leak through and become amplified.

Balanced lines have two audio signal carrying wires wrapped by a separate shield wire. The shield protects the inner wires from excessive noise pickup. And because the inner wires are carrying the same signal at equal levels, they are said to be balanced. **Fig. 8-3**

BALANCED AND UNBALANCED LINES

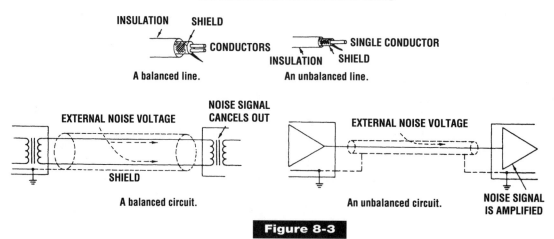

Figure 8-3

Balanced and Unbalanced Input/Output

Just because balanced cables are used does not insure quiet operation. The input circuitry must be balanced as well; that is, capable of receiving a balanced line. Understanding balanced inputs can be best understood by describing common mode rejection.

There are two basic types of balanced inputs, transformer and electronically balanced. Both operate on the same principle with each having advantages. The principle of common mode rejection is that the input device will not pass a signal if it is common to each wire. The obvious response to this is: "Isn't the audio signal itself equal level on each wire?" Although they carry the same signal, remember it is an alternating current - while one wire is positive, the other wire is negative. So at any instant, the signal on one wire is 180 degrees out of phase with the other, therefore, the input passes the signal.

Extraneous noises, however, will be present on each wire at the same time equally. Stated another way, the noise is common to both wires and the inputs will not pass it. This is accomplished by two terminals receiving the audio signal and the ground being connected to the chassis.

An unbalanced input, like an unbalanced line, has one terminal for the inner audio signal carrying wire and another terminal receives the outer wire which has two functions, the other audio signal, and the shield for the ground. This type of input is used on the inputs of all guitar amps.

CABLES AND CONNECTORS

Because of the use of components in sound reinforcement equipment, several different type of connecting cables are necessary. Cables are the most common cause of sound system problems. The choice of an incorrect or faulty cable can create severe sound degradation or perhaps no sound at all. Differences in cable include the number of conductors, shielded or not shielded, thickness, and type of wire used.

The wire used in portable audio cable should always be stranded not solid. Shields should be made from braided wire not foil (Foil actually is a better shield but is more fragile). Balanced lines require cable with two conductors wrapped by a shield, a total of three wires. Unbalanced cable means only two wires, usually one conductor wrapped by a shield.

All low level and line level devices should be connected with shielded wire to help prevent noise from entering the system at this stage. This is critical because noise mixed with signal at low and line levels is yet to be amplified. That means that any noise will be amplified to greater volumes too.

Connections of the high level type (power amp out to speaker in) should use unshielded cable for two reasons. First, that noise entering the system at this point will not be amplified and will not be noticed over the signal. Second, shielded cable adds resistance and capacitance which deteriorates the quality of sound over long cable runs. Also, many power amps will not work well with the high capacitance of shielded cable.

There are several different types of connectors used on audio equipment. Each type has male and female version. The most common connector is the 1/4" phone plug named after its developer—Ma Bell. One quarter inch refers to the diameter size of the shaft. The phone plug has two different configurations. The Tip/Sleeve (TS) plug is a two wire plug used for unbalanced operation. The other configuration is the Tip/Ring/Sleeve (TRS) plug and is used for three wire connections. This TRS plug can be used for balanced operation or for two discrete signals with the sleeve connection being the common ground. The 1/4" plug is often used for its small size and reasonably dependable operation. **Fig. 8-4**

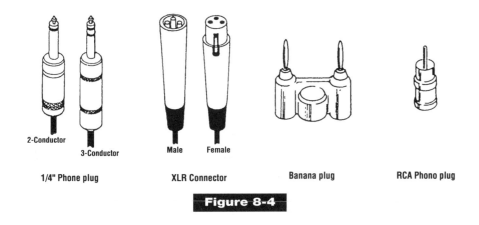

2-Conductor
3-Conductor   Male   Female

1/4" Phone plug   XLR Connector   Banana plug   RCA Phono plug

Figure 8-4

A more dependable connector is the XLR or "Cannon" plug. It is a three pin plug and is used for balanced operation of low level or line level devices. It is also becoming more prominent in speaker connections due to its locking ability.

Banana plugs are another type of connector used for high powered signals. They are more desirable in connecting high powered speaker cabinets because of their high current handling capacity.

"Speakon" connectors manufactured by Neutrik feature high current capabilities and provide a twist and lock function to prevent accidental pull out.

Another common connector in audio systems is the RCA phono plug. This type of plug is usually used on tape recorders, stereos, and other hi-fi equipment. Because they are fragile, they are usually not found on sound reinforcement equipment other than in adapters.

There are adapters made for every audio connector in almost any configuration. They do no alter signal level or impedance. They simply connect one type of plug to another.

A Working Example

Now that we have some of the theory of impedance and signal matching explained, consider the following equipment and determine whether they are all compatible:

Sam, our hypothetical "engineer" from Silly Sound Company has installed a new mixer, power amp, and speakers at a night club. The owner insisted however, that Sam use his old style passive equalizer and an old open reel tape deck left over from the old system. He also reused the 22 gauge speaker cable because the speakers were mounted on the ceiling beams and Sam was too lazy to run new wire.

The club reopens and Sam's best friend Bob is going to run sound for the band that night.

Here is a look at the system setup:

Looking at microphone #1, this lead singer "eats" the mike and sings loudly. Note the level of peaks from the microphone is -10 dBv which is about .3 Volts. During sound check Bob set the input gain at 40 dB of gain. A little math shows that 40 dB = 100 times something; so .3 V x 100 = 30 Volts. This shows that at the input the pre-amp is trying to put out 30 volts, which it can not do, so the singer's voice will be distorted. Also because the channel is so "hot", the channel fader is pulled way down and has hardly any control movement left. Too bad this board didn't have input peak LEDs.

Microphone #2 is in front of a guitar amplifier and the pre-amp gain was set at 26 dB of gain. 26 dB = 20 times something so multiplying our microphone output by 20 gives us a 6 volt peak which the board can take. However, the guitar player wants to patch a cheap foot-pedal effect into the channel and it has a maximum input level of 1.5 Volts so on peaks it's over-driven.

Looking at the output of the mixing board, the output impedance is 130 ohms and the EQ that is connected needs to "see" a 600 ohm source. As a result of this impedance mismatch (rare these days), the EQ is not working properly and has dips and peaks in the frequency response. So Bob has his hands full with feedback problems.

Earlier Sam had set the output of the mixer to read "zero" indicating a +4 dB output (1.23 V), and turned the level of the power amplifier so it would reach clipping at +18 dBv to allow for 14 dB of headroom. However, Bob came by and turned the power amp level control fully up thinking he would get more volume. Now the power amp will clip when it receives .5 volt input (about –3 dBv) Bob found that he had to keep his master fader way down or else he would get distortion. As a result, his output meters were barely registering. Because he ran unbalanced cable from the EQ to the power amp right past the air conditioning units, hum was increased 21 dB louder.

Sam had wired one set of speakers with new 14 gauge cable, but used the old 22 gauge wires on the other set. The new wires total .26 ohm which makes the total impedance of the load on that channel 1.56 (three 4 ohm speakers + .26 ohm of the cable). Since our power amp puts out 500 watts at 2 ohms, the amp will try to put out about 640 watts into the 1.56 ohm load. So, the power amp is distorting and is getting hot which means the thermal protection is about to kill the power.

The cable represents 16% of the total load (.26/1.56) and multiplying that by the output power (640 watts) shows that 106 watts are being wasted in the cable.

The other channel of the power amp has 1.3 ohms of speakers in series with 200 feet of 22 gauge cable. The wire has 6.6 ohms of resistance, so the total impedance on the channel is 7.9 ohms (let's call it eight ohms). At eight ohms, the power amp is putting out 200 watts of which the wire is wasting 83% or 166 watts. The speakers are getting only 34 watts! No wonder Bob thinks his speakers are blown.

When the band breaks, Bob starts the old tube-type open reel tape deck for background music. Sam had connected it to one of the extra "mike" inputs which has 1250 ohm input impedance. The recorder output is attenuated by the mismatch from the normal .25 Volt output down to .006 Volts, and also is distorted.

While Bob goes over to phone Sam for advice, what can be done to correct the situation?

Microphone #1:

Bob needs to turn down the trim control at the input. If the mixer had an LED input light it would be easy to tell where to set it. Since we don't, it must be set by ear.

Microphone #2:

The foot-pedal effect should not be used here, however, if the band insists, he will have to turn down the gain control to keep the output level under 1.5 Volts. Again since we don't have a peak light on the mixer, we can use the peak light on the effect. If the effect does not have one, we need to set levels again by ear. We will probably run into some noise problems with this channel.

Mixer Output:

Bob needs to add 470 ohms of impedance to the output impedance of the mixer. This can be accomplished by simply wiring a resistor of that value into the connector itself. Use of this resistor will attenuate the mixer's output but that could be adjusted back in at the power amp or at the master fader of the mixer.

Power Amp:

Sam's original idea of calibrating the amp was correct. Bob shouldn't have messed with it. This calibration allows the user to read from the board how much power he is putting out. This will also help prevent the excess noise from the air conditioner.

Speakers:

Sam has too many speakers hooked up to the amplifier. He needs to get another amp or use fewer speakers. He should also use much heavier gauge speaker cable.

Tape Recorder:

The problem with the tape deck was it went into too low an impedance. This could be solved by using a direct box or line level transformer with an input impedance of at least 100K ohms (preferably 500K). Note that even the high impedance input at 10K ohms would not be suitable for the 50K output impedance.

Mixers

The major goal of a sound system is to bring together all the audio signals and blend them. This is what we hear when we listen to a recording, a group of instruments "mixed" together. It is important for a mixer to have good performance specifications but it is equally important to be designed with usable features and logical layout.

Before describing the features and functions of a mixer, it is best to take a look at how to follow the signal flow. This is accomplished with block diagrams.

UNDERSTANDING BLOCK DIAGRAMS

The design of every electronic product requires a schematic diagram which shows every component from input jack to transistor to the AC line cord. This diagram is used by a technician to trouble-shoot and repair the equipment. There is another type of drawing called a block diagram which traces the signal path and allows the user to understand the different functions. It also aids in determining hookup and other applications.

The features of the equipment are represented by symbols and the signal path is illustrated by arrows and lines. Here are some standard symbols: **Fig. 10-1**

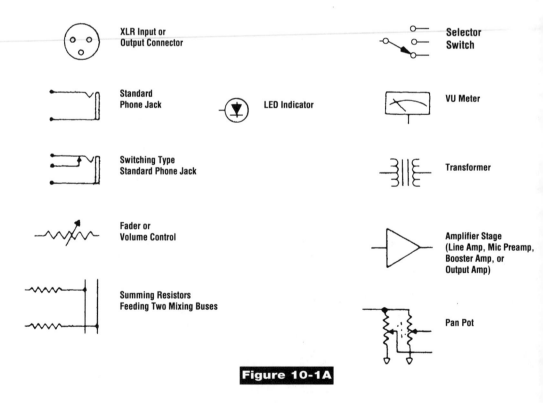

Figure 10-1A

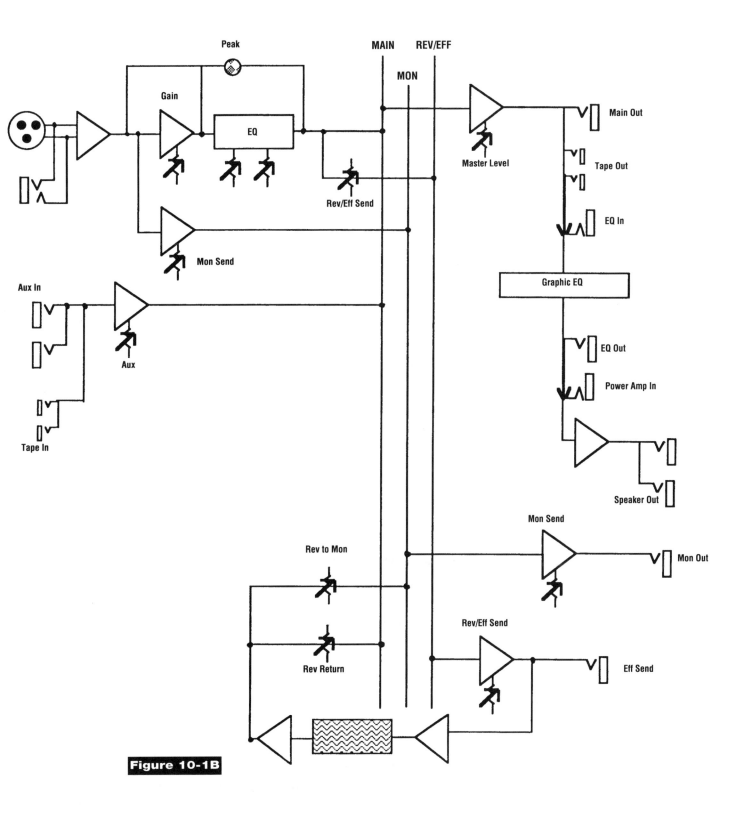

Figure 10-1B

FEATURES AND FUNCTIONS OF MIXING BOARDS

Input

The most common type of mixer inputs are 1/4" phone jacks and XLR female connectors. These jacks are used to facilitate sources fitted with either style of plug. Most mixers designate the 1/4" phone jack as a high impedance input, while the XLR connectors are used for low impedance sources. The inputs accept a wide range of impedances as well as signal levels. The XLR jack is usually (but not necessarily) a balanced input. The 1/4" input could be balanced if a Tip/Ring/Sleeve (T/R/S) jack is used, but they are usually unbalanced.

Signal Matching to Pre-Amp

To compensate for the wide range of signal levels, many mixers have a TRIM control which allows a proper amount of signal to be sent to the pre-amp. If a strong signal source is used on a mixer without some type of TRIM control, distortion could occur. If a weak source was used, the mixer would require so much added gain that noise or hiss would develop.

Depending on the mixer, this function is achieved by variable attenuators or slide switches. A variable attenuator allows more precise setting, thereby increasing the signal to noise ratio.

Peak Indicator

If the input stage is over-driven, distortion will occur. Sometimes it may be difficult to determine exactly which input is distorting when many signal sources are being used. The peak LED indicator eliminates the guesswork. It illuminates when the input is approaching the clipping or distortion level. Occasional blinking is permitted, but if a more steady light occurs, the TRIM for that channel should be readjusted to reduce the level.

Channel Patching

It may be desirable to add an effect device such as a compressor or a noise gate to a single channel. Some mixers offer a patch point which takes the signal out of the signal path, allowing signal processing before returning the effect processed signal back into the path This is achieved by either separate send and return jacks, or by using a stereo 1/4" phone jack. The stereo jack has three terminals, a send (either on the TIP or RING), a return (the alternate used from the send), and a common ground for both (SLEEVE). This type of connection is called normalled. That is, if no plug is inserted in the jack, the signal will flow through the normal path. However, once a stereo plug is inserted, the signal will leave the path on the RING and return on the TIP connection.

Channel Equalization

Tone controls on a channel are used to accentuate the subjective sound qualities of the source. The amount of control over the sound is determined by the amount and type of tone circuits.

The area of frequencies affected by active tone controls can be varied. Shelving EQ's begin their rise (or fall) at a particular frequency and eventually flatten out, or shelve, at some other frequency. The amount of boost or cut is rated in dB. The point at which the curve boosts (or cuts) 3 dB is the action point of the curve. For instance, a mixer's LOW EQ has an action point of 500 Hz, but a maximum boost (or cut) of +/– 12 dB at 80 Hz. This means noticeable tone changes begin at 500 Hz, but the shelving takes place from 80 Hz on down. **Fig. 10-2**

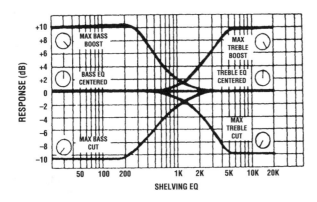

Figure 10-2

Peaking EQ's have a selected bandwidth and will boost or cut a certain number of dB around a center frequency. This type of EQ is usually used to alter mid-range frequencies. **Fig. 10-3**

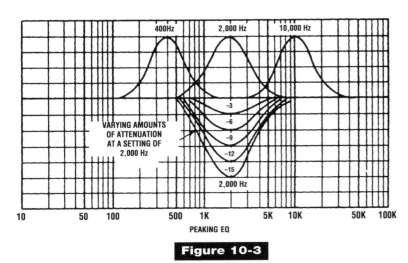

Figure 10-3

With Parametric EQ's you have the ability to select the desired centered frequency with a Sweep control. It also has a control allowing adjustment of the bandwidth (also known as "Q"). Instead of a peak EQ covering the area of an octave, the "Q" control can narrow or broaden that bandwidth allowing further customizing of the signal.

Fig. 10-4

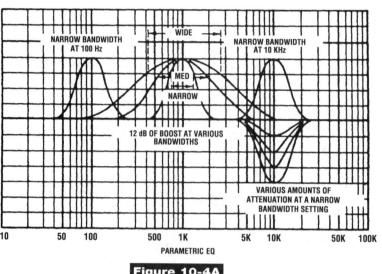

Figure 10-4A

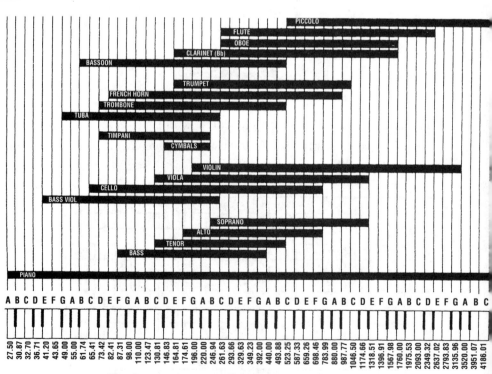

The frequency range of various musical instruments

Figure 10-4B

Many boards use high and low shelving EQ's which allow general boosting or cutting of upper and lower frequencies. If more control is needed, a third band of EQ covers the middle frequencies, usually in the form of peaking curves.

Equalization should be used carefully. Excessive use of the tone controls can yield an unnatural or noisy sound. Remember, if the input is a guitar, it should sound like a guitar. It is very rare to need more than a 6 dB boost or cut for the majority of instruments. **Fig. 10-5**

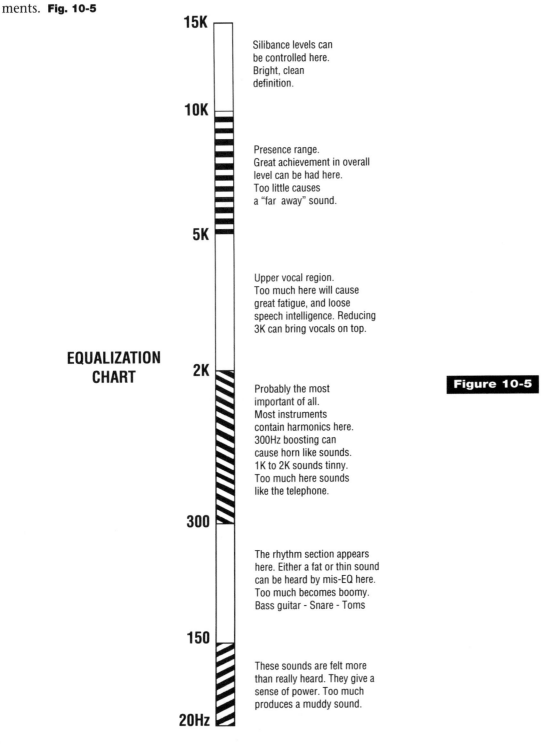

EQUALIZATION CHART

Figure 10-5

15K — Silibance levels can be controlled here. Bright, clean definition.

10K — Presence range. Great achievement in overall level can be had here. Too little causes a "far away" sound.

5K — Upper vocal region. Too much here will cause great fatigue, and loose speech intelligence. Reducing 3K can bring vocals on top.

2K — Probably the most important of all. Most instruments contain harmonics here. 300Hz boosting can cause horn like sounds. 1K to 2K sounds tinny. Too much here sounds like the telephone.

300 — The rhythm section appears here. Either a fat or thin sound can be heard by mis-EQ here. Too much becomes boomy. Bass guitar - Snare - Toms

150 — These sounds are felt more than really heard. They give a sense of power. Too much produces a muddy sound.

20Hz

Boosting tone controls can also add gain to the pre-amp. If too much boost is applied, clipping may occur requiring the resetting of the TRIM control.

Channel Volume

The overall level of the individual channel is controlled by the channel level or volume control. This is the control used to balance or "mix" the inputs. This can be accomplished by rotary controls, but many mixers use slide potentiometers called faders. The faders are desirable in that they allow more than one channel to be moved simultaneously, they are easier to operate than rotary controls.

Bus

A b s in electrical work is a piece of copper or aluminum wire used to connect all collective fuses to the main power. A bus in a mixer connects all the channels to an output. A mixer can have several buses to assign the signal from each individual channel to other grouped areas. Common buses include Sub buses, Main bus, Monitor buses, Reverb/Effect buses.

These separate signal paths allow the input signal to be split off from the main signal path at different areas to be used for different reasons. Most buses have level controls, either rotary or slider, which allow proper level setting in order to minimize noises and distortion.

Monitor Bus

Many mixers have a monitor bus which is used to send the signal to the stage for on-stage "monitoring" of any or all of the inputs. It may be desirable to hear a particular input in order for the on-stage musician to perform better.

This bus should be split off before the channel level (pre-fader) because the level for the main speakers may not be desirable for the stage or monitor area.

Sub Buses

A so-called stereo mixer is so named because it has two main buses labeled left/right or Sub1/Sub2. A channel can be assigned to either or both sub-masters by means of a PAN control. The pan control gets its name from the movie business where "to pan" means to move a camera from one side to another. In a mixer, you can pan the main signal from a channel from one main bus to the other.

This assignment allows similar inputs like vocals or instruments to be grouped together and controlled by separate volume controls (sub-masters).

Sum Bus

A stereo mixer (one with sub buses) should have a sum mixing bus which simply is the combination of the left and right sub buses. This controls the overall level of the mixer when used in a monaural mode.

Reverb/Effect Bus

Many mixers have on-board reverb which can be assigned to any or all of the inputs by means of the channel REV/EFF SEND. This bus takes the signal after the equalization and after the fader (post-EQ, post-fader) and sends it back into the Reverb device. After the Reverb, the signal is dumped back into the main bus to be mixed with the original signal.

This bus can also be used to assign the post-EQ, post-fader signal to an output which is used for connection of a signal processing device such as a delay or a chorus unit. This affected signal can be returned through an effect return input, an auxiliary input, or even through another input channel. Regardless of the return input chosen, the affected signal needs to be mixed with the original signal.

Outputs

Like the inputs, the outputs use 1/4" jacks and XLR connectors and are almost always low impedance. Typically the 1/4" jacks will be unbalanced and the XLR will be balanced.

A mixer with power built in will also have 1/4" jacks for the speaker outputs. Only speakers should be plugged into these with unshielded cable.

Master Equalization

Master equalization sections, available on some mixers, operate like channel equalization in that they affect the tone of the signals in that mixing bus. They differ, however, in that they are broken down into narrower frequency ranges, allowing much more control over the tone setting. They also differ in that they affect the entire mix rather than one signal.

Graphic Equalizers are the most often used in master equalization. Graphic EQs are a series of peaking EQs, each covering a different frequency area. The range of frequencies or bandwidth is the same on every peak. This type of device uses sliders covering individual bands. It receives the name graphic EQ because the user can graphically see the frequency alteration he has selected. **Fig. 10-6**

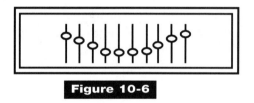

Figure 10-6

Because they affect the entire mix, master EQ sections should not be adjusted listening to only one source. They should be adjusted to improve the overall sound quality of all the inputs. This is similar to adjusting the tone controls on a home stereo. The bass control affects the bass response of everything heard, from the drums to the guitar to the lead singer. **Fig. 10-7**

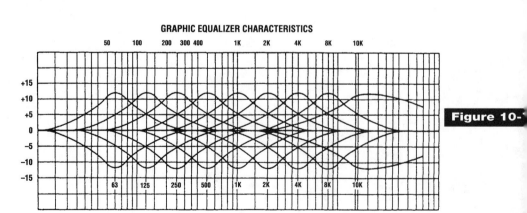

GRAPHIC EQUALIZER CHARACTERISTICS

Figure 10-7

MASTER EQ METHODS

It is common practice to adjust a graphic EQ so it looks like a smile. This is done because we do not hear frequencies equally. However, arbitrary setting to a "smiley face" is incorrect. Because it does not take into account room acoustics. There are three primary methods of setting master equalization.

1. **By Ear.** This is the most cost effective method of setting master EQ however it has severe limitations. Because quality of sound is subjective and varies by listener, there is no one correct setting. In order to set an EQ by ear, do the following.

   Listen to the source acoustically and try to get to sound natural.

   Use a familiar program source (cassette, CD) and try to get it to sound like what you are used to hearing.

   Avoid any excessive boosting or cutting.

2. **Feedback Tuning.** This method utilizes a flat response, omni-directional microphone. Plug the microphone into any unused, un-equalized channel. Turn up the gain and volume of that channel. With your graphic EQ set flat, slowly bring up the overall system level. A frequency will start to ring. (Be careful not to let this ring excessively or speaker damage may occur) Pull down on the EQ slider that makes the feedback stop. Pull only a few dB, not all the way. Increase the system gain again and another frequency will begin to feedback. Pull down on the corresponding EQ slider again. Repeat this procedure three or four times only.

   After that, go to the sliders you have not yet moved and bring up their level until that frequency feeds back. Continue this throughout the remainder of the slider you did not originally touch. It is important to note, once you have completed this you are not finished. The EQ you have just added brings the speaker to a flatter response for the room. You must then add subjective equalization to improve the overall sound. (See below)

3. **Real Time Analyzation.** A real time analyzer uses pink noise to "flood" the room with sound and record the findings on a graph. **Fig. 10-8** Pink noise is noise with equal amounts of energy between each octave. So the energy in the octave 200–400 Hz is the same as 3000–6000 Hz. The line should appear flat on the graph. Any peaks or valleys should be remedied by the EQ until flat is achieved.

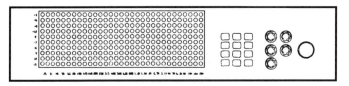

REAL TIME ANALYZER

Figure 10-8A

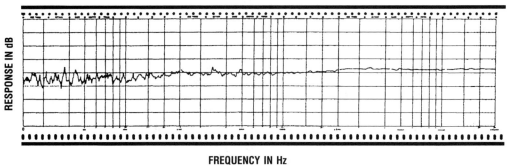

FREQUENCY IN Hz

Figure 10-8B

In both feedback tuning and real time analyzation, the end result created equal sound at all frequencies in the room. However, we do not hear all frequencies equally so additional EQ may be necessary to create a desired overall sound. One such "preferred curve" is actually a series of boosting and cutting at various frequencies so the human ear hears all frequencies at the same level. These curves are known as the Fletcher-Munson Equal Loudness Contours. **Fig. 10-9** Notice that the amount of boosting changes with overall listening levels. That is because of the ear hears lower frequencies better as volume level increases.

After you have achieved an electronically flat response from your speakers in the room by either feedback tuning or using an RTA, then add the equalizing specified by the Fletcher-Munson chart. It is important to find out what sound pressure level you will be performing at so as to choose the right curve.

The Fletcher-Munson Equal Loudness Contours are only a guideline for "preferred" sound. Experimentation in any band's "preferred" sound is completely subjective.

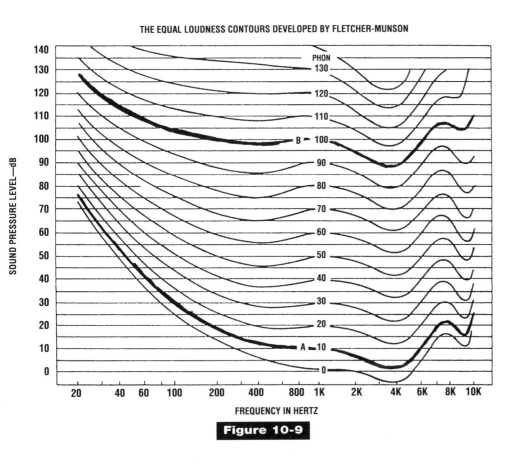

THE EQUAL LOUDNESS CONTOURS DEVELOPED BY FLETCHER-MUNSON

Figure 10-9

UNITY GAIN

In addition to setting channel and master equalization, another critical point to running sound is setting proper signal levels. This can be accomplished by a technique called unity gain. There are several stages in a mixer where the signal can be amplified: at the input, at the channel, and where the channels are grouped together in the master section. At each of these areas gain must be maximized in order to obtain a good signal to noise ratio and to prevent distortion. We will take each section separately.

In order to set levels, it is necessary to send a signal through each channel being set. this can be accomplished by singing into a microphone in that channel or playing an instrument which is plugged in. If a microphone is used be sure to sing in a stage voice, not a meager "check, check."

At the input of many mixers is a switch or rotary control labeled trim, attenuation, input level, pad, or gain. This control adjusts the level of incoming signal so it is acceptable to the pre-amp. If too much signal enters the mixer, distortion will result. If this occurs, the mixer operator needs to reduce the incoming signal level with the Trim control. If a weak signal enters the mixer, signal should be boosted or else there will be excessive noise mixed with the signal.

Many mixers feature an LED light for this input area to notify the operator when the input signal is correct. If this light is constantly lit, too much signal is overpowering the pre-amp and distortion is present. The light should flicker occasionally on the loudest music peaks. If the mixer does not have an LED light, input level setting must be done by ear. (It can also be accomplished with a volt/ohm meter or by reading the mixer's output meters but this is much more difficult.)

Adding excessive equalization on a channel may also trigger the input LED peak light. If this occurs, the trim control must be reset or equalization should be reduced. Conversely, if the equalizers are greatly reduced, more gain should be added via the trim control to compensate for the drop in signal level.

The control which determines the level or volume for each channel usually does not add gain, but merely reduces the level that is there. This volume control should not be turned up all the way for starters, however, or else there will be no way to make that channel louder. The volume control should be set at a level where the operator can boost or cut volume during the performance. On many mixers this nominal operating area is designated by 0 dB or some graphic element indicating a normal operating level. If the mixer is not labeled as such, turn the volume control halfway up. This will allow boosting or cutting as needed.

If a powered mixer is used, there is usually a master volume control which determines the level of signal being sent to the internal power amplifier. This amount of signal can usually be determined by an LED or VU meter. This master volume control does not have to be set at nominal. Instead, it should be set to the desired listening level for the room.

If an unpowered mixer is used, the unit must be calibrated to the external power amp used. If the power amp has an input level control, it should be turned fully down. The mixer should then be turned up to a desired maximum operating level (indicated by the LED meter) for when the amp should produce full power. Then turn up the level control of the amplifier until full power is reached. This will be indicated by an LED peak light, Limiter light, or LED/VU meter.

If the power amp does not have an LED which indicates power output, or if you have a power amplifier which has more output power than your speaker can handle, another method can be used. This method requires a volt/ohm meter and a little math.

First, calculate the amount of power you wish to send to your speakers and calculate the total impedance of all speakers used. Then, using the Ohms Law equation, calculate the necessary voltage.

$$E = \sqrt{P \times R} \quad \textbf{where} \qquad \begin{aligned} &E = \textbf{Voltage} \\ &P = \textbf{RMS Power} \\ &R = \textbf{Total Load Impedance} \end{aligned}$$

For example, suppose you had two 8 ohm speakers which could handle 100 watts RMS each and a power amp that could produce 1000 watts into 4 ohms. The two 8 ohm speakers would form a 4 ohm load that could handle 200 watts RMS. Those are the numbers to plug into the equation.

$$E = \sqrt{200 \times 4}$$
$$E = \sqrt{800}$$
$$E = \textbf{28.28 Volts}$$

28.28 volts is the amount of voltage the power amp should produce to give you 200 watts into those two speakers.

Connect the volt/ohm meter to the output terminals of the power amp. Set the meter to read AC volts on the 10–100 Volts scale. With the mixer set at your desired maximum output level, turn up the level control on the power amplifier until the volt/ohm meter reads 28.28 Volts. Do not operate the mixer past your maximum output level or else you will be sending more than the 200 watts which is what the speakers can safely handle.

Monitor Systems

The purpose of a monitor system is to allow the on stage musicians to hear themselves in order to perform better. The typical problem with monitor systems is that the musicians would like to have loud, high fidelity sound, but because of physical positioning and space limitations this is not always possible.

The biggest cause of a poor sounding monitor system is operator error because of lack of knowledge. There are many steps to take to achieve a proper monitor system and the best way to obtain a good sound is to eliminate the problem.

Here are some commonly asked questions:

"Every time we try to turn up the monitors to the level we need, we get feedback." The most common cause of feedback in the monitor system is microphone placement. All microphones have a published pickup pattern known as a polar response. An omni-directional microphone picks up signals from every direction. A cardioid microphone has a pickup pattern that looks like a heart. Notice that as you go "off-axis" from the cardioid microphone, it doesn't pick up signals as well. There are several cardioid microphones, each with their own polar response pattern. Notice that the super cardioid pattern has minimal pickup at 150 degrees, while a hyper cardioid and regular cardioid have minimal pickup at different angles.

This is why some musicians place one monitor directly in front of them and others have one or two monitors off to a side ahead of them. The best way to find where the monitor to mike pickup is least is to experiment with one monitor and one mike.

"Ok, that sounds logical, but we have only two monitors and five singers spread out all over the stage." In this case, there has to be some planning done to find out strategic microphone and monitor placement. First of all, the microphone with the worst front-to-back pickup ratio will feedback first and that will be as loud as that mike will get. The best solution is to use similar microphones and to group musicians as close together as possible. Another solution is to buy more monitors.

"Remember, we need our monitors loud." One common problem bands run into is that the stage volume of their amplifiers is too loud. This causes a number of complications. First, the power needed to be heard over the stage level is enormous, especially if a few monitors are used. Another is listening to loud volumes for extended periods of time causes the threshold of hearing to shift up to accommodate the loud level. This will cause AMP WARS; the need to turn up your amp on stage to be heard over the other guys. By this time, the monitors (and your ears) cannot keep up with the levels and the overall sound heard in the audience is very unbalanced.

The best thing to do is either mike up all the instruments or play at a level where you are not damaging your ears and insulting the audience. There is nothing wrong with loud music if it is achieved correctly. By the way, after the threshold of hearing shifts upward, it will come back down, but never to the level it was before. This is a form of permanent hearing loss.

"Our monitors always sound funny." This could be the result of over-equalization. The most common equalization used on a monitor system is a 9 or 10 band graphic EQ. The problem with using this type is that severe boosting or cutting of even one band (fader) can make the overall tone unnatural. This is because a single band covers such a wide range of frequencies. Subtle changes can rid the system of feedback, yet still preserve a functional sound. Another alternative is to use a notch filter or different type of EQ.

FEEDBACK

Anyone who has used any sound reinforcement equipment has experienced feedback. Feedback is the annoying squealing sound that occurs when a microphone is turned up too loud or is placed in front of a speaker. Although feedback is rather complex, it can be understood as certain frequencies becoming resonant and being reproduced infinitely. Feedback takes place when a sound source (microphone) picks up a frequency it is sensitive to and keeps reproducing it in an infinite loop. **Fig. 11-1**

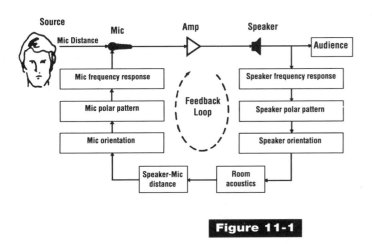

Figure 11-1

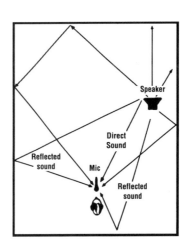

Because feedback is caused by certain frequencies, it can be eliminated electronically or acoustically. The most common method of eliminating feedback is with a graphic equalizer. When a suspect frequency begins to "ring", a band on the equalizer can be reduced. The problem with using graphic equalizers is that they alter a wide range of frequencies and excessive reduction can yield an unnatural sound.

A better solution is to use a narrow band equalizer or a notch filter. This operates on the same premise as a graphic EQ except the range of frequencies affected is much narrower.

Parametric equalizers can be used by setting the bandwidth or "Q" control on its smallest setting, cutting the level control and dialing in the suspect frequency.

In all the above solutions, the ringing frequency had to be determined by the listener's ear. This usually meant trial and error of selecting different frequency bands. There is a unit called a Real Time Analyzer which displays the audio spectrum on a screen and allows visual monitoring of feedback.

A less expensive approach to solving feedback problems is using acoustic solutions. This can range from moving a speaker to pointing a microphone in a different direction. Feedback occurs because of reflecting sound waves reentering the system. If this can be prevented, feedback problems are minimized. Here are some ways this can be achieved:

1. **The most effective way to get a microphone louder without feedback is to increase its gain (output).** This is accomplished by miking close—stand near the microphone. Also, mike the loudest part of an instrument. You get more signal from the sound hole of a guitar than you do the bridge.

2. **Keep microphones away from speakers.** Never point a mike at a speaker because the microphone becomes more sensitive to the feedback threshold. Always keep the main speakers in front of the stage microphones and keep them as far away as possible.

3. **Use directional microphones.** Microphones have certain pickup patterns and can have very good rear rejection. This means only sound from directly in front of the microphone will be picked up.

4. **Use similar microphones.** A chain is as strong as its weakest link, and if feedback occurs at a certain level with a cheap mike, that's as loud as that microphone will get. This could throw off the balance of the entire group.

5. **Use as few microphones as possible.** As the number of microphones increases, the amount of gain before feedback decreases.

6. **Use direct boxes and pickups.** A direct box is a transformer which allows a line level signal from an amplifier to be sent directly to the mixer. This device usually converts from high impedance unbalanced to low impedance balanced. Contact pickups can be used on acoustic instruments such as pianos and guitars and allow more gain to be achieved.

7. **Place speakers toward the rear of microphones.** When using floor monitors, aim the end of the mike into the center of the speaker. This will minimize pickup of the speaker's output into the microphone.

8. **Use a smooth response microphone.** Microphones with large peaks tend to feedback easier at those frequencies than smooth response mikes.

9. **Add absorptive material to the playing area.** Minimizing sound wave reflections by hanging carpet, towels, or some other sound absorbent material.

Grounding

We are all familiar with AC 3-prong into 2-prong adapters. The biggest problem with them is that no one uses them correctly. If the wall outlet has only two prongs and no adapter is available, everybody knows the solution: break off that long third pin, right? **WRONG!!!** There is a reason equipment manufacturers use those three pin AC plugs. That reason is grounding. Grounding audio equipment is important because it prevents shock hazards and eliminates external noise.

As the name suggests, if current gets on a wire that is grounded, that current will go into the ground—Mother Earth. Ideally, everything is grounded into the Earth. Equipment requires two wires to operate on AC, a hot and a neutral. The hot is the 110 volts in your house. The trouble with this two wire system is that if a fault or short circuit occurs, a shock hazard is present. An example of a fault would be a lead from the hot accidentally touches the chassis of a piece of equipment making it "hot" as well.

If a third wire (ground) is used, it is always attached to the chassis. If a fault condition now occurs, the hot signal is sent down the ground wire into the Earth. This open circuit usually causes excess current and will probably blow a fuse.

This is the theory behind grounding for safety but other problems exist. What happens if the AC receptacles are improperly wired? If the ground on the receptacle doesn't really go to "ground", the third wire on the AC plug is fairly useless and voltage can appear on the chassis if a fault occurs. The hot and neutral wires can be reversed, also causing potential problems.

The best way to eliminate the risk in plugging in equipment is to buy a three prong outlet tester. **Fig. 12-1** This device is very inexpensive and simply plugs into the wall socket. Three LED lights indicate if the socket is wired properly or warns of what type of problem exists.

Another problem is a two wire AC receptacle. If there are only two slots in the receptacle, the outlet cannot be grounded, right? Not necessarily. The three prong into two prong adapters were made for this reason. **Fig. 12-2** The two prongs match up to the hot and neutral wires and the ground is made with that wire or clip on the adapter. The adapter's ground wire must be connected to a true ground like the ground inside the receptacle. You can verify the ground and correct wiring with the three prong outlet tester. If the polarity of the wires is reversed, simply reverse the adapter in the receptacle. Also, be sure that the ground is properly wired in the outlet. The tester will indicate this.

We have described the safety precautions of grounding single pieces of equipment, but since sound reinforcement consists of many components, the entire system needs to be grounded. A common shock problem occurs when the musician completes a circuit. This happens when a mixer is correctly grounded but another piece of equipment, say a guitar amplifier, is not properly grounded. A microphone in the mixer is grounded but a guitar connected to the amp is not. If the musician touches the strings of his guitar and the microphone at the same time, dangerous AC voltage could be present which could kill the musician.

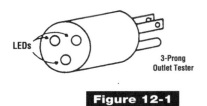

LEDs

3-Prong
Outlet Tester

Figure 12-1

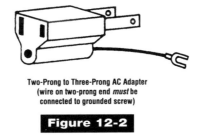

Two-Prong to Three-Prong AC Adapter
(wire on two-prong end *must* be
connected to grounded screw)

Figure 12-2

Although the primary reason for grounding is safety, improper grounding can lead to excess noise in the system. An example of poor grounding is a "ground loop". This situation occurs when two pieces of equipment are plugged into different AC outlets. Because the ground is common to both, the chassis are linked. When a cable is used to connect audio signals to these components, a loop is formed. This loop is susceptible to external noise pickup. **Fig. 12-3**

At first it may seem logical to lift the safety ground on either piece of equipment. While this will terminate the loop, the hazard of shock now exists. The best solution is to use a common AC receptacle and to run the AC power cords close to each other.

Another cause of a ground loop is patching through the effect send and return. Because the ground is common to the mixer and the effect, a loop is formed. This noise induced into the system by this loop can be reduced by keeping the cables as close together as possible.

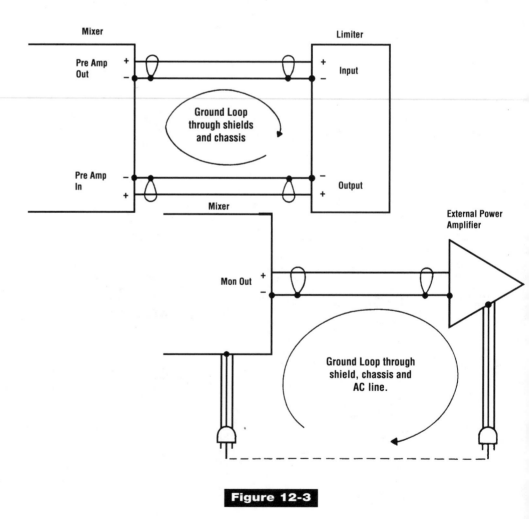

Figure 12-3

Lights can be a cause of noise in the system as well, especially when dimmers are used. To help solve this problem, try to run the lights on a separate AC circuit. You can tell if it's a different circuit if it has a different fuse or circuit breaker. If you have no access to a different circuit, make sure that the dimmer circuits are properly loaded. That is, if the dimmer is rated at 1000 watts, use 1000 watts worth of lighting. You can also install filters at the dimmer circuits to eliminate the noise.

Some tips on reducing noise include:

1. **Keep cables short.** Running short cables reduces the area of the ground loop.

2. **Keep cables of the same type close together.** Run AC cords, line level cords, low level cords in separate groups. This eliminates loops.

3. **Keep cables of different types away from each other.** Keep power cords away from microphone cables, line level cables away from speaker wire, etc. If you have to cross different types of cable, cross them at 90 degrees. That will reduce the chance of hum entering the system.

4. **Rack mount your equipment.** The metal rails of a rack ground the chassis together as well as keeps the units close, allowing use of short cables.

5. **Use proper cables.** Using a shielded cable for a speaker can degrade the sound quality and performance of the power amplifier. Always use shielded cables for low and line level signal and use unshielded cable for high level signals. Use balanced cable whenever possible. Remember, a faulty cable is the number one cause of unwanted noise.

6. **Be sure to match signal levels.** Hiss can occur in a system if the output of one device is too weak for the input of another. Know the input and output capabilities of the equipment used.

Glossary

A-B TEST
Evaluation of comparative performances of two or more amplifiers or speaker systems by switching quickly from one to the other.

AC or ALTERNATING CURRENT
Electric current with periodically changing polarity.

ACOUSTIC ABSORPTION
Sound deadening characteristics of any substance. A "Sabin" is a reference unit of absorption equal to sound "absorbed" by one square foot opening through which sound passes (never to return).

ACOUSTICS
Pertains to act or sense of hearing, science of sound, or sounds heard. Anything relating to, containing, producing, arising from, actuated by, or carrying sound.

ACTIVE
A type of circuitry that can decrease or increase the amplitude or gain of a signal.

AMPERE
Unit of measurement of electrical current (A).

AMPLIFIER
Device capable of increasing the magnitude or power level of a voltage or current that is varying with time (frequency), without distorting the wave form of the signal. The amplifier in "signal amplifier." The incoming signal from any program material source is too weak to power a speaker system. Amplifiers strengthen the weak signal to a power level that operates loudspeakers with minimal distortion.

AMPLITUDE
This is another term for "level" or "volume" of an electrical or acoustical signal. A measurement of the height of a wave form.

ANALOG
An electrical signal whose frequency and level vary continuously in direct relationship to the original sound waves. "Analog" may also refer to a control or circuit that continuously changes the level of a signal in direct relationship to the control setting.

ATTACK
Beginning of a sound or the initial transient of a musical note.

ATTENUATE
Reduce the level of an electrical signal, usually with a volume or loudness control. Also, to reduce sound levels acoustically with absorption material.

AUDIO FREQUENCY
Any frequency within the range of normally audible sounds, roughly from 20 Hz to 20,000 Hz. (Hz=cycles per second.) sound waves from interfering with its front wave.

BAFFLE
Panel within an enclosure that the speaker is mounted on. This term is derived from its primary function: preventing or baffling the speaker's rear sound waves from interfering with its front wave.

BALANCED
An audio circuit with three wires. Two wires carry the signal (high + low –), the third is a shield connected to a chassis or system ground. The signal leads are both of equal potential difference from the ground, and are "balanced" relative to the ground. Improperly referred to as "floating."

BALANCED LINE
A transmission line made up of two conductors plus a braided shield, capable of being operated so that the voltages of the two conductors are equal in magnitude (voltage) and opposite in polarity to the ground.

BANDWIDTH
Refers to the "space" in the frequency response of a device through which audio signals can pass (between lower and upper frequency limits, those points where the signal level has rolled off 3 dB).

BASS
The low audio frequency range, normally considered to be below 500 Hz.

BASS REFLEX
Type of speaker enclosure in which the speaker's rear wave emerges through a vent or port to reinforce the bass or low frequencies.

BI-AMPLIFICATION
In a conventional sound system, the full range audio signal passes through one amplifier and feeds a high-level crossover within the speaker that divides the audio to feed the low and high frequency drivers. In contrast, a bi-amplified system uses a low level crossover or electronic crossover to divide the full range audio signal into two parts for feed to two separate power amplifiers, one for low and one for high frequencies. The output of the high frequency amplifier feeds the high frequency driver and the output of the low frequency amplifier feeds the low frequency driver.

BLOCK DIAGRAM
Schematic-like drawing illustrating the main circuit blocks and signal flow in an electronic device or system, but not showing all specific wiring details.

BREATHING
A phenomenon sometimes heard when a compressor is used to control a complex program signal, or even a single voice in the presence of background noise. "Breathing" is a modulation of the background sounds. Because a strong signal is absent, the compressor's gain increases, causing the background sounds to become louder. The compressor then reacts to the strengthened signal by weakening it, resulting in the perceived breathing effect. Breathing is usually undesirable and can be reduced by altering the attack and/or release time of the compressor, and by using no more compression then necessary.

BRIDGING
Connecting one electrical circuit in parallel with another. Example: paralleling power amplifier inputs.

BUS
A conductor that serves as a common connector to several signal sources, always associated with a mix amplifier.

CAPACITOR
Electronic device that passes AC currents and blocks DC currents. Also used to store voltages. A capacitor is made of two metallic surfaces divided by an insulator.

CARDIOID
Microphone with a heart-shaped pickup pattern more sensitive to sound projected to its front than its back.

CASCADE
An arrangement of two or more similar amplifier stage circuits in which one stage directly feeds the input of the next.

CENTER FREQUENCY
The frequency where the greatest amount of boost or attenuation (cut) occurs in a peak/dip-type equalizer or a notch filter.

CLIPPING
Occurs when the capabilities of an amp are exceeded. The resulting sound is distortion, and is visible on an oscilloscope.

COMMON MODE REJECTION
Ability of an amp to cancel a common mode signal (such as interference) that is applied equally to both ungrounded inputs of a balanced amp, while responding to an out-of-phase signal.

COMPLEMENTARY CIRCUITRY
A push/pull power amp utilizing both P-N-P and N-P-N type output and driver transistors to obtain low distortion.

COMPRESSION DRIVER

A high frequency transducer whose diaphragm (dome) is designed not to radiate sound directly into the environment, but instead to be coupled to the air more efficiently by means of a horn.

COMPRESSOR

An amp that decreases its gain as the level of the input signal increases to reduce the dynamic range of the program. It may operate over the range of input levels, or it may operate only on signals above or below a given (threshold) level.

CONDENSER MICROPHONE

A microphone utilizing a capacitor as a pickup element. Electronics are usually contained in the microphone body and a polarizing voltage is necessary, so external or battery power is required. Output levels are usually higher than other types of microphones. They are commonly used for high quality audio applications.

CONTINUOUS

This power rating is representative of the most conservative rating of an amp's power. It is also called "RMS" when amplifying a constant steady tone. It is usually measured at a signal frequency of 1000 Hz for a specific distortion.

CROSSOVER

A device that separates the audio signal into two or more frequency ranges. Crossovers can be active or passive. ACTIVE are designed to split line level signals and are used before the power amps. PASSIVE are designed to split high level signals and are used after the power amp. These crossovers are usually located within the speaker cabinet.

CURRENT

The rate of flow (measured in amperes) of electricity in a circuit (I).

CYCLES

A unit of motion referenced to a period of time, usually one second.

CYCLES PER SECOND

The number of completed vibrations designated by: equilibrium, compression, and rarefaction, or by positive and negative swings. This is also known as Hertz (Hz).

DAMPING FACTOR

A measurement of how well an amplifier controls the movement of a speaker by preventing it from shooting out too far. Damping factor is determined by dividing the speaker impedance by the amplifier's output impedance. The higher the damping factor of an amplifier, the greater its ability to control the speaker's movement.

dB or DECIBEL

A unit of measurement for describing the ratio between two voltages, currents, or powers. Based on logarithms, decibels eliminate the use of large numbers. Decibels are only useful when referenced to a known value.

dBu

Is an electrical measurement of power. 0 dBu is equal to 1 milliwatt or 1/1000 of a watt, which is the same as .775 volts across a 600 ohm impedance. +30 dBu is 1 watt, +50 dBu is 100 watts.

dBV

Is an electrical measurement of voltage 0 dBV is equal to 1 volt. +10 dBV is 20 volts.

DC or DIRECT CURRENT

An electrical current of constant polarity. DC travels only one direction unlike AC (alternating current) which alternates directions/polarity.

DECAY

The fading of a sound after its attack.

DELAY

A device that delays an audio signal by a certain length of time, usually up to 1 second. This delay can be accomplished in one of three ways: ANALOG uses an electronic process that stores the actual signal voltages. DIGITAL operates electronically through a binary number storage process that represents real analog signal voltages. TAPE uses magnetic recording and simply plays back the recorded signal.

DIRECT RADIATOR

Any loudspeaker not horn-loaded. Usually a cone speaker mounted to a baffle.

DISTORTION

Any change in the audio signal causing the wave form to appear differently at the output than at the input. There are several types of distortion.

DISTORTION, HARMONIC

Distortion signals that are whole number multiples of the input signal. In individual measurements can be made for each harmonic (2nd, 3rd, 4th, etc.), and are usually specified in a percentage (%) or in dB below the fundamental frequency.

DISTORTION, INTERMODULATION (IMD)

Distortion signals that result from the interaction of at least two input signals. The distortion components are not harmonically related and are usually more objectionable.

DISTORTION, TOTAL HARMONIC (THD)

The sum of all harmonic distortion components in a signal. Usually measured as a percentage.

DISTORTION, TRANSIENT INTERMODULATION (TIM)

Intermodulation distortion that occurs only momentarily during brief signal peaks or transients.

DYNAMIC MICROPHONE

A microphone that converts acoustic energy to electrical energy through a moving coil around a fixed magnet.

DYNAMIC RANGE

The difference, as perceived by human ears, between the loudest and quietest portions of a musical performance. Measured in decibels.

EFFICIENCY

The ratio between the energy output and the total energy input. For example, an average speaker may be 3–5% efficient, meaning the speaker loses over 95% of the electrical energy sent to it. Efficiency should not be confused with sensitivity which measures sound pressure level of the speaker.

ENCLOSURE

An acoustically designed housing structure for a speaker.

ENVELOPE

The moment to moment changes in signal levels of a program. Refers to how notes start, sustain, and stop.

EQUALIZATION

The manipulation of tone by increasing or decreasing frequency ranges through tone controls, filters, or equalizers.

EXCURSION

The extent or measure of a loudspeaker's cone movement.

EXPONENTIAL HORN

A speaker component designed to reproduce high frequencies. An exponential horn has a flare that increases at an exponential rate.

FADER

A potentiometer that controls the signal level in a mixer's channel. Can be rotary or slide control.

FEEDBACK, ACOUSTIC

The regeneration of a signal from the output that reenters the input and can cause a squealing sound.

FEEDBACK, ELECTRONIC

Part of an amplifier's design that returns a portion of the output signal to the input. Increases stability and reduces distortion.

FIDELITY

A term to describe the accuracy of recording or reproduction of audio processing.

FINITE BAFFLE

A type of cabinet with opening that allows the rear wave of a loud speaker to exit. Usually, the back of the cabinet is open.

FLETCHER-MUNSON EQUAL LOUDNESS CONTOURS

Graphs that depict the amount of boost frequencies required for the human ear to hear them equally. Levels of boost change as loudness increases.

FREQUENCY

The change in the air pressure (sound) or the change in voltage (electricity) in a given period. Measured in cycles per second (Hertz), also used to describe musical pitch. The higher the frequency, the higher the pitch.

FREQUENCY RESPONSE

The range of frequencies a device will produce or reproduce. Frequency response should also list a variance; i.e., 20–20,000 Hz +/–6 dB.

GAIN

An increase in signal strength or amplitude usually specified in decibels.

GROUND LOOP

A condition when two or more devices have a path to a common ground and voltage is unequally induced in each unit. A ground loop also forms when two or more devices are connected in such a way to create a large magnetic field inducing noise or hum into the system. This magnetic field can be developed spaced connecting cables or connecting cables and ground wires.

HARMONIC

Integer multiples of a fundamental frequency that are generated because of the actual construction, components and design of the unit. The first harmonic is the fundamental frequency, the second harmonic is twice the fundamental, the third harmonic is three times the fundamental, etc.

HEADROOM

Headroom refers to the difference between the nominal operating level and the maximum level at any point in the audio system.

HERTZ (Hz)

The unit of measurement for frequency, also known as cycles per second.

HORN

A flared or funnel-shaped device connected to a driver to more effectively couple sound to air. There are many types of horns. **FRONT LOADED** refers to the front wave of the speaker exiting the horn. **REAR LOADED** refers to the rear wave of the speaker exiting the horn, with the front wave exiting through a port. **FOLDED** refers to a long horn designed for low frequencies and then made more compact by a series of folds. **EXPONENTIAL HORN** is any horn where the flare rate follows an exponential curve. **RADIAL HORN** utilizes a compression chamber and curved inner surfaces to create a wave that is a section of a sphere. **CONSTANT DIRECTIVITY** maintains its frequency response throughout its dispersion area.

IMPEDANCE

The total opposition to the flow of alternating current in an electrical device measured in ohms. Impedance can be measured at the source and at the load.
SOURCE IMPEDANCE (also known as OUTPUT IMPEDANCE) is the impedance inherent in the signal source such as the output of a microphone or amplifier.
LOAD IMPEDANCE (also known as INPUT IMPEDANCE) is the impedance "seen" by the signal source to this input. For example, if a speaker has an input impedance of 8 ohms, the power amplifier will "see" 8 ohms.

IMPEDANCE MATCHING

Refers to the proper connection of devices. When the output impedance of a source device is acceptable to the input impedance of another.

INDUCTOR

A device (usually a coil) inserted in the circuit to oppose the flow of high frequencies.

INFINITE BAFFLE

A cabinet design that does not allow the rear wave to exit the cabinet.

INPUT LEVEL

Refers to a device's acceptable signal input. Rated by maximum level (above which distortion would occur) or nominal level (the average level sent to the input for normal operating conditions).

INSERTION LOSS

The reduction of signal level caused by the insertion of an electronic device (such as a tone filer) in to the signal path.

JACK

A receptacle for connection of a cable's plug.

LED

Light Emitting Diode. A device that emits light when current flows through it. Often used to indicate signal level.

LEVEL

The value of a signal relative to a given reference, expressed in decibels. A term used to describe signal strength or amplitude.

LEVEL MATCHING

(See signal matching.)

LIMITER

A device that puts a ceiling or limit on output level regardless of input level.

LINE LEVEL

Signals operating around +4 dBu or 1.23 volts.

LOAD IMPEDANCE

(See impedance.)

LOGARITHM

The number to which the base number 10 must be raised (not multiplied) to express a number as an exponent ie: 10x10=100
Log10 100 = 2

LOUDNESS

Sound level as perceived by the human ear, known as Sound Pressure Level. The human ear will hear different frequencies at different levels.

MASKING

A phenomenon where one or more sounds can "trick" the ear into not hearing sounds that are simultaneously present.

MIX

The technique where two or more signals are combined and balanced on a piece of audio equipment.

MIXER

A device that brings signals together to be level balanced and processed before being sent to additional audio equipment such as power amplifiers and speakers.

NOISE

Any unwanted signal in the audio mix such as hiss, hum, RF interference, etc.
Different types of noise include:
PINK NOISE, a random noise modified to have equal energy in each octave. Although 10,000 to 20,000 Hz has 10,000 different frequencies, it is modified to have the same amount of energy as the octave 200 to 400 Hz which contains 200 frequencies.
WHITE NOISE is random noise with equal energy for any equal bandwidths. For example, the frequency range between 5,000 and 10,000 Hz occupies a 5,000 Hz bandwidth. The frequency range between 10,000 and 15,000 also occupies a 5,000 Hz bandwidth. Because the octave of 10,000 Hz is 20,000 Hz, it contains twice the energy as the 5,000 to 10,000 Hz octave, therefore, white noise increases 6 dB per octave as frequency raises.

NOTCH FILTER

A type of equalizer which cuts out or "notches" a very narrow band of frequencies.

OCTAVE

An octave is the doubling or halving of a frequency. For the frequency 1,000 Hz, one octave up would be 2,000 Hz; two octaves would be 4,000, while one octave down would be 500 Hz.

OHM

A unit of measurement for resistance. One ohm equals one volt divided by one ampere.